Mythology
the
Science of Myth

★

essay

★

Traumear

Paperback ISBN 978-0-244-97222-6

*

www.traumear.com

*

The spirit today is myth and myth is the spirit, let us repeat that. Today is not a day that will one day be yesterday, but today is the day in which we live now, and we are live today, not extinct.

World as mythology reveals its innermost secrets, and this is in fact the use of mythology, that it leads us, gently and persuasively, to the heart of that realm where everything that is wanted may be gained merely by asking for it. Also it teaches us how to ask, so that we do not waste time and energy asking for wind when we want power and asking for flame when we want warmth or heat.

Far too many of us have made up our minds as to the means to happiness and we ask for those means instead of asking for happiness. So it matters a great deal how we prepare ourselves for the times ahead.

The worst fate is not to love and then not to know we are loved, because then we have no myth as nourishment and none to protect us. Myth nourishes, it repairs, sustains and increases, when we love nonetheless.

*

The Science of Myth
or
Mythology

Where myth is concerned we like to surround our-selves with abstract defenses. These defenses, as soon as we recognize them, are then consciously adopted and so they become altruistic themes. As such they do service for a while. We may not understand exactly how this works at the time, but the important thing is that it works, while it does, and when it stops working we think again.

The production of natural causes, through the ages, and their reproduction as art works, eventually comes to be understood initially as historical process, and finally as a line of development with beginning and end. The understanding we invest in this whole accumulation of things, usually seen in the round through the eyes of con-temporary genius, lets us deal both creatively and criti-cally with ideas and realities on a par, so that we make no distinction any more between thought and feeling, be-tween natural man and human nature, except perhaps to illustrate certain discrepancies in the past and to show how they had cropped up due to such a distinction.

Now mythology, which is knowledge of a kind, and in particular knowledge for the sake of understanding myth, can be practiced in various ways, and certainly what counts for one person at a time, for me or for you, is that at least one such way is practiced, and it would be absurd to 'pretend to wish to absorb them all'. This has been done from time to time and it must be rejected, since it is based on the false assumption of a finite state of real and true happiness.

Similarly the question as to what myth is, so that we may understand it, if we are not immediately struck by the ridiculousness of it, can at least be seen to be wrongly applied, and the best that can be said for it is that it urges us, by default, in the direction of a regular and comprehensive point of view on this matter so that we may begin again with a sound application of sense.

Myth is of course, by definition, that beyond which we cannot see and whoever disputes this fact obviously has something else in mind. The unlimited senses are not the ones we are born with and they are not the ones we hope to die with, so the least we can do is admit that somewhere along the line a break takes place, an interruption of our everyday faculties during common knowledge or as we rise to the occasion of whatever challenge is put in our way.

Such a break in sensation – call it the evil that comes into the world, if you like – affords us a very profitable starting point for mythology indeed. Evil, as a nuisance, basically, can be dealt with mythologically, and in order to cope with it in earnest we require a sense of humour.

*

Myth as fact:

The ordinary sensations of which men are capable, a red car travelling down the street, the indefinite roar of a machine somewhere on earth or in the sky, a clock ticking or the suggestion formulated by high heels on hard pavement, fresh air and fried trout on a meadow behind Mount Temple in the Rocky Mountains – all these are facts and I can vouch for them, but as facts they have become myth. No one would dispute the fact that they have become myth, because to do so would mean questioning one's capacity for love, one's willingness to realize in created surroundings a similitude and a tolerance of name.

We could also say that a name is given for the sake of eventual myth, but then we should add right away that myth does not wear out but at best it is worn in. Facts as such may leave us in the lurch for a while and we may wonder had we got them right or did we do our best by them, and facts of course share with many other things, due to their possible plurality, their capacity for relative importance. Certain facts may not matter to me at all right now, but they may in a moment. Others, insofar as they have attained to a factuality of sorts (which always depends on their degree of human use) may be important for me without my knowing it. But there is no plurality of myth. There can be no concrete evidence of such a thing and the critical spirit in its turn will not allow it. Myths, like religions, are indigent fantasies of criticism, or due to criticism.

A reason for distinguishing between myth and fact may be the need to raise fact to the level of myth, and such a need should never be trifled with, especially not in children. Intellectual curiosity is never in itself sufficient reason to make the distinction and in addition to dismally failing, it also desperately misleads, most commonly due to a demand for allegiance to one against the other. But then where myth is acceptable as such it can never be de-based, and where it has been worn in, as we phrased it earlier, it can not any more be cast off. The thing about myth that changes is its taste, its quality and its character, though never along a scale of values; not better or worse, but a different taste, another quality and alternate character. The aspect of myth cannot even be the same from one person to the next, which makes out its peculiar strength. Like colour in a painting, we would never disagree about it, though we might discuss the paint or argue about pigment. Disagreement on essentially differing aspects is out of the question. Materials are brought together and facts arise, but a chronicle of facts has nothing to do with myth.

A permanent barrier against myth-creation is put up by those who insist on a relevance between myth and the status quo. The life of a nation, for example, precludes the principle stimulus towards myth because it parades as sufficient response to an individual's highest aspirations. Only where those aspirations can find evidence of themselves in human actuality, here and there, and not in popular conceit, can myth as a type of spiritual nourishment thrive. By popular conceit we mean all those flights into nuance and detail where the central intelligence has been neglected or gone astray.

The acceptance of the status quo, whether personal or political, is important, even critical, but as raw material, not as a form or as the shape for things to come. To begin with things precisely as they are at the moment, this can only be seen in the light of realistic practice. But we shall need to get to know our moods, our temperament and the pattern of our organic behaviour. These correspond naturally to the taste, quality and character of myth as we previously indicated, and so we have acquired an objective leverage for our study of myth in the making.

Myth in the making :

Suddenly we have an inkling of what it means to be faced with the need for survival. How we respond to that need is entirely up to us but we may do it mythologically. Consequently we interpret the need rather than identifying with it. One interpretation of it may lead us in the direction of a natural image, where we calculate what it is we want from what we imagine we require. Such a calculation satisfies because it instructs our faculties without laying any moral obligation on us. For example :

A man and a woman may get together on economic grounds in the hope that this will give them an edge in the race for prestige in the local community. After a while they feel trapped, success is not forthcoming. Children are seen as impositions and intruders, work loads as burdens that infringe against liberty by increasing boredom. One recognizes a need to survive. An interpretation of this need allows the man to behave as husband and the woman as wife. One refuses to inquire into definitions outside such conduct and meets terrifying problems in a merciful way. The terror is described in terms of itself, the mercy becomes available along with one's singular dedication to one's growth as husband or wife. The systematic acceptance of duties in relation to the children is transformed because husband and wife automatically behave as father and mother, where the children are seen as opportunities first and foremost. Finally there is the myth of the family, which embraces parents and children as equal members, susceptible to similar sentiments and sharing in a common goal. Fatherhood, motherhood and childhood are experienced as what they are, which is mythic entities, and not played as roles or pursued as sacrificial consequences to some detrimental end. Manhood is worked out by the man as a husband and womanhood by the woman as a mother. Manhood and womanhood are also part and parcel of the mythic context. They are not separate myths. Within this context the man and the woman find rest. This means that they are able to live life to its fullest.

The making of myth, then, rises out of an interpreted need for survival.

Basic to the interpretation is the calculated option of a freedom from need; central to it is the operation, directly on survival as an idea or an ideal, of the will in its function for critique.

A need to survive springs up in our mind when it feels threatened in its autonomy. As soon as we identify with such a need, we feel threatened ourselves and 'suffer from the will to survive', in other words we want to survive. This falls into a category, along with wanting to be an individual, wanting equal rights, etc. and at the heart of it beats a life-excluding contradiction.

A need to survive can also occur in our body of course, when it separates itself off and takes matters into its own hands, as it were, so that we begin to behave like a machine. Again we do well to guard against this, and when we find ourselves struggling to derive justification from external causes, we can go ahead and act automatically in order to get ourselves out of a tight spot. Any usual bad habit of insisting on derivative instances of our previous experiences, no matter how sweet and seductive it has become for us, must be forcibly overcome if mind and body are to be one again for ourselves.

The most dangerous need to survive arises like a contagion in our soul. Here we feel emptied of all sense, and nothing seems to matter but a frantic domination, by the will, of our environment. Here especially it makes little difference whether we speak of 'the' will or of 'our' will because the distinction has become negligible, obviously due to an eclipse of our intelligence. The scheme laid out for our activity implies nothing except fierce willfulness and brutality. Actually we should welcome such a unique configuration of potentialities because it affords us also the greatest leverage for the making or receiving of myth. But such opportunities arise and exist where and whenever a need to survive occurs, so that responsibility and watchfulness can be seen to go hand in hand.

A need to survive contains opportunity and a risk factor but a will to survive is downright dangerous. While the former may be interpreted, in line with various illusions and facts at our disposal, for the sake of its specific content in terms of class and originality, the latter must be countered immediately by a will to live. Let us keep in mind however that a will to survive amounts to an identification on the spot with a need to survive, so that we are not dealing with disparate concepts.

But a will to live is essentially self-critical. I recognize a danger and make myself responsible for an alleviation of the circumstances that lead to a catastrophe. This making of myself responsible, in both senses of the word as cause and effect, brings me into contact with the very substance of myth, and it only remains for me to undertake appropriate action for myth to be complete.

A will to live, in critical counterpoise to a will to survive, goes on to interpret a need to survive wherever we come across it. Such a critical interpretation elucidates states of mind, explains moods, clarifies emotions and motivations, points to significance where it crops up and generally creates a more lasting veneration for life in all its diverse forms and sizes. The process itself is mythic. The substance of myth becomes part of us and we become part of it. We may regard ourselves as human beings with a name.

*

The substance of myth:

The substance of myth is most readily available as language, in speech or writing, but it is also immediately accessible or innately 'at hand'. If we want to make use of it for our own ends primarily, we have no need for language, since language, after all, is the source of communication. Means of communication, by the way, are words.

If we discuss language at length we are bound to gain insight into the substance of myth, which we may also call mythic substance. Remember that it can be tasted and touched, that it can be eaten and digested, and that humanity as such is made up of it insofar as we refer to it as human being. This is explained in the sentence that *humanity is the essence of being*, and the crown or fruit of humanity is a human being.

A human being is the most precious thing. That this being has language is both wonderful and marvellous but the use of language does not come readily to a human being. It despises itself as soon as it participates in another human being and so it tends to avoid language so that it might isolate itself in reflection and contemplation. Considering the definition of a human being this is hardly surprising. But in isolation achieved arises the sense of community, and this sense then naturally seeks its own object, just as the eye seeks light. The approximation of a state of isolation therefore is required before communality as a concept attracts us. Then we accept language as a godsend and we interpret any further isolation as a waste of time.

Let us therefore not waste anyone else's time by insisting on language where a human being still waits to be reminded of its isolation from within. Language based on grammar would be such a waste of time, while language in the service of oneself may always be held out, 'at hand', in case a human being is ripe for maturity.

As language flows from us, we ourselves become mythic substance. We do not differentiate anymore now between myself as a human being and ourselves as human beings except as suffering souls. Where we suffer, so that our passions are involved, we still become unique, each to himself, though never in isolation. This is because a degree, at least, of human or mythic substance has passed into our being and so we may be alone but never separated.

Where we touch mythic substance we begin to comprehend one another. But it will not suffice to seek; we must act. Now language as an act will not readily come to mind because most of us have become accustomed through the years to think in terms of language rather than in terms of thought, and consequently we distrust language unless controlled by us rationally, or spontaneously thrown away in talk. For language even to be conceived of as an act it must be understood that a critical awareness of ourselves, while we communicate, is possible and highly recommended; not a critical awareness of our language, of what we say and how we say it, but indeed of ourselves, which critical awareness assures that our language remains whole. To the extent that we become entangled with our communication we lose track of it as a sensible thing or an articulate process and indulge in fatuity or deal in fallacy. Only hypocrisy is required to make these two sound important with style. Style after all is no respecter of persons, and neither does it wait to be invited before making its appearance, so we need to look further afield for a guarantee of worth.

We do in fact have such a guarantee where we act in spite of a total critical self-awareness. Such an act then cannot have anything about it, anything that would distract or inhibit, or in any way distress that upon which we act, and since it does, after all this, amount to action, it cannot fail but must succeed.

A total critical self-awareness may be brought to bear on the occasion of intentional love. The language of love therefore would seem a most suitable specimen for action at any cost, and we know that in a crisis nothing succeeds like love – depending on what we love. So in the present case we love the substance of myth. But how can this make any sense?

The problem arises where we confuse substance with matter. Matter can always be pictured and significantly pointed out. It allows itself to be transformed and transferred; we can guide our ships and rockets in terms of it and it supplies us with a momentary respite on our way from one station of life to the next. Where matter becomes an aspect of survival, addictions to forms of it take place and soon there is talk of vices, sins and crimes.

But substance is neither visual nor in any sense contractual. Therefore, unless we cherish extinction in the past, we must endow our substance with a name and with only one name, and this is the one name available for the substance of myth : Jesus.

*

The myth of Jesus:

By Jesus we mean Jesus of Nazareth who lived and was killed many years ago. That he did in fact live once may be accepted on evidence from what other people say and have written down or it may be rejected, if we assume that stories were invented and then taken for fact. One is free to accept or reject a fact. This means that we have the benefit of the knowledge of that fact or else we do not. It does us no actual harm to reject a fact.

It does do us actual harm however to reject the substance of myth called Jesus. This is so because it happens to be part and parcel of our human make-up. It always has been.

The point we wish to stress at the moment however is that myth exists prior to its essential manifestation as fact and that it is of primary importance. Whether or not we

11

accept the fact is up to us, as we mentioned, but our ability to accept it depends in the first place on the very myth from which it forms an expression. As a matter of fact even the strength we need to reject the fact, though not its application, depends on, and goes out from, the mythic primacy of that fact, so that by the misapplication of an original life energy, if I may put it that way, we cut ourselves off from the beneficial reward right now.

Fact is of secondary importance, and if we describe it as something that actually happened or something that really exists we may, through time, tend to forget or neglect to mention the dual aspect of its nature. To impose a unity or oneness on facts or the factual is to do a disservice to ourselves as factual beings, whether we have in mind a unity of purpose, of origin or of fashion.

That the essence of a fact, and the essence which is a fact, is twofold, and how it is twofold, or why, cannot be argued but only perceived. Only in the perception of facts as dual entities can we draw from them their general utility or endow them with their particular currency and force. Our senses themselves are twofold, in correspondence to perceptible fact, and if we were to conceive of sensation as a singular thing we would be translating it into the realm of myths, where, far from becoming myth itself, it would partake of a kind of supernature and become invidious or vicious.

When we study a fact we take advantage of its dual nature to help us make the myth sensible and palatable. Even controversy, which contradicts the duality of facts internally, may have this end, though not necessarily, because when controversy becomes an end in itself, as when it supports one aspect of factual knowledge to the detriment of what then becomes 'its opposite', again in the hope of a unitary fact, it creates a fallacy.

So the opposite of fact is fallacy, and a fact can only be opposed, or opposite, to another fact, in the interest of mutual distinction and integrity, not for the sake of annihilating it or doing it down.

As for a fallacy, it can only be dropped; one cannot argue against it from some standpoint of fact because that supposes a common basis or assumes a possible point of overlap. A fallacy is dropped in the interest of fact, and in order to assist in this one can only again stress, emphasize or repeat the relevant fact, and this in the fullest cognizance of its dual nature.

Through the factual apprehension of myth, which is a perception of facts in their twofold nature in order to attain myth substance, we incorporate into our being an analogue of Jesus, and this analogue of myth substance leads us and guides us then, on the road to the union of myth and fact.

It cannot help us to keep myth and fact separate and distinct. Where we come upon facts we do well to perceive them as such, for the purpose of myth substance; where we come upon myth, let us render it factual, for the sake of all those who have not come upon it yet and in order to deepen our own roots in it : and where we are not in the clear as to whether we have one or the other, myth or fact, no attempt in the world to distinguish one from the other, or to decide which it is we have, is going to succeed, because such an attempt would be ill based upon a presumption of our own factual predominance or mythic superiority.

Clarity about the issue of 'whether myth or fact' can only be gained within the perceiving organ or achieved from beside the actual deed. Whether one or the other, makes no difference, but that it must be one or the other, in any case of unclarity, is of the essence.

Let us assume for example that we cannot make up our mind as to whether the resurrection of Jesus, as we understand or experience it at the moment, is mythic or factual. We suspect there may be some of both in it. What we have picked up from books and in classrooms and by word of mouth from our next of kin and friends, from priests and preachers, leads us to propose for our inquiring faculties, including the faculty of belief, a kind of tripartite riddle : matter has decomposed, appearances have become spirit, god has become flesh. At the same time we become aware of an urgency from within to quarrel with the alleged equivalence of those concepts, of a compulsion to invent, from first causes, a picture of resurrection as we ourselves would have managed it if we had been possessed of a kind of magic or miraculous powers, and in addition to this we feel most originally constrained to sustain a critical individuality, in the face of everything really, our own urges and compulsions included. We would resent and regret any infringements of our sense of honesty, our personal integrity, our various paradigmata of conscience, (of which we have, since childhood, collected more than a few, though some may have accumulated more on account of a lack of awareness than due to wakefulness, but more of that another time). At the same time we have a powerful and primitive thirst for justice, a will to do the best we can, a desire to be free and happy, in other words to be fully and completely ourselves.

On one side of us stand those who urge us to 'look at the facts' – as they see them. On the other side stand those who tell us a story and ask us to believe it – their version of it. There is only one way out, and this is usually a way that incurs criticism from both sides, sticks and stones from left and right. It is the way through our own personal conception of fact as we do conceive at that moment, through our own characteristic proposals of myth as we can propose them at that moment. Either one or the other, in sufficient quantity or to a sufficient extent will see us through our predicament, and we will have ended by becoming and having done what we saw initially only as an external problem and an impersonal challenge or threat.

In our present case, this occurred as an example of the resurrection of Jesus.

So it happens that when we try to separate myth from fact we destroy the fact and discredit the myth. Reasons for wanting to facilitate such a separation fall into one of two categories. Either one is dissatisfied with oneself or one is unhappy with circumstances. We propose to treat these two separately, as they do in fact occur separately, and to show how each one may lead to a common fallacy regarding myth and fact.

*

The absence of Jesus:

Dissatisfaction with myself is a common occurrence; it happens nearly every day, to a lesser or greater degree, and it seems to take a certain amount of courage to even recognize that this is the case. Physiological disturbances, without the intervention of a careful intelligence, cause physical and mental disturbances, quite mechanically, and these try to correct themselves organically through reactionary behaviour. But as soon as I countenance such a physiological disturbance, within myself, I immediately occur to myself as in some sense a failure. No one, including myself, actually likes to be reminded of this. Only after much practice of understanding do we eventually arrive at the point where we welcome right quickly such a disturbance as a herald of good things to come. In our present inquiry however we want to diagnose how a lack of proper understanding leads us into the fallacy of wishing to separate and distinguish myth from fact. A critical diagnosis such as this maintains its awareness of a state of soundness while limiting itself intentionally to the recognizable factors of the ailment.

A critical diagnosis of self-dissatisfaction as a mistaken interpretation of physiological disturbances : this is how it looks at the moment, and one would like to persuade the reader to accept this frame of reference.

The assumption of such a thing as a self is fallacious in the first place. A number of unpleasant sensations draw me into their sphere of effectiveness – of affection – and suddenly I am not any more myself but a self. A subtle change has taken place and a change for the worse, no doubt. This self, endowed right quick with a psyche, poses as me, as myself, and I am willing to take this pose for a genuine characteristic of my own. It pictures itself for me, this self, and I am glad to take this so-called self-image for an authentic personality trait.

Now of course such a self is a lie through and through, but I accept it because it makes certain promises, holds out benefits such as relief, consolation, peace and rest. In short, it masquerades as that which it is not.

But we would be quite mistaken to assume in retrospect that such a lie of a self begins to exist in any way independently or separately from our own consent to it or to its promises. The very possibility of such an independent self as a convenient and workable curtailment of our troubles rests entirely with ourselves from the start. There is no such thing as a devil or demon except insofar as we encourage the manufacture of it, by itself if you like, out of nothing.

Prior to our consent to evil there is no evil.

Separate from our involvement in evil there is no evil.

And these two rather simple insights lie at the heart of our inquiry. Because we encourage, nourish and foster the self, this lie to which I consent, into which I have half-consciously slipped, turns now to the light of day and requires a recognition there, since like all things, true or false, it craves reality. All things, good or bad, eventually come to the light of day and face reality. But reality is a mix of myth and fact; available equally in one or as the other. (Whether we walk willingly or are dragged against our will is entirely up to us.) Now when my self is confronted by this mix of myth and fact, it requires the

17

usual sanction of an emerging thing out here, but due to its own one-legged make-up it can only afford to buy one shoe, even though shoes come always and everywhere in pairs. It wants to cut myth off from fact so that it can appropriate one of these two to itself and reject, at least for the moment, the other.

An attempt at self-realization in response to self-dissatisfaction, through the medium of a self : this is how we can understand, as compassionately as we choose, any desire to see myth separate from fact, any wish to distinguish the two, any undertaking to render them discrete. But reality is wonderful, and while it remains possible for all of us to destroy this wonder for ourselves, happily we cannot harm it in reality.

Perhaps one should add here, as a cautionary note prior to our analysis of how our unhappiness with our circumstances goads us into a fallacious interpretation of reality as a separation of myth from fact, that whether we see reality as myth or as fact makes little difference, as long as we do not try to see it as myth rather than fact, or as fact rather than myth; as myth to the exclusion of fact, or as fact at the expense of myth.

An unhappiness with our circumstances we usually notice first of all not so much as a physiological disturbance, as in the case of self-dissatisfaction, but as an inhibition of our practice. We want to do but cannot. The contradiction tends to drive us out of ourselves, out of our mind and body, and before we can say what has happened, we have fastened to some aspect of our environment, mental or physical, in the hope of overcoming our inhibition there. Again it has to be stated that we can arrive at the point, through much wisdom as insight, where such an inhibition, even after we have externalized it, can strike us fairly soon as an adventitious event and as a harbinger of good influence, but here we want to limit ourselves to an analysis of the wrongdoing we permit ourselves when we proceed blithely from the fear of a catastrophe to a sectarian point of view on the world, in the deluded hope of cleansing ourselves in this way of the imputation allegedly due to our surroundings.

Once again, the unhappiness occurs when we desire to impress our personality on our environment and find ourselves thwarted and frustrated. Not that our environment as such has gone missing but rather its accessibility to our faculties and its susceptibility to our tools. The customary procedure from means to end has broken down. In the past a certain device has always led to a definite result, but not any more. A cause and effect relationship that has always been dear to us refuses to hold. A child whose obedience we have come to take for granted not only refuses to obey but acts as though it were totally unfamiliar with the concept of obedience. A world that has always responded to our flattery not only treats us with contempt but refuses to see why this should surprise us.

The practical effectiveness has gone out or our lives.

We make ourselves responsible for a mechanical substitute for this effectiveness.

And here we have the problem in a nutshell. Where once cause automatically led into effect, we now attempt to make the effect follow the cause mechanically. The means is not any more original to the end but has come to stand outside of it. And in both cases it finally seems to depend on us and on our power to close the chain, to manipulate the sequence and to activate the program. Napoleon sees himself as the lynchpin that ties a revolutionary people to the idea of a European monarchy. Faust in Goethe's tragedy considers it increasingly his role to activate, to propagate and to stimulate, so that others might prosper. Both try to make up for a lack of natural consequence by becoming themselves either an end or a means, either a cause or an effect, one or the other, and whichever one they isolate for themselves, the other one they see as their environment, separate and distinct from themselves. A permanent sanctioning is now required for this fallacious view of life as a case of activity now, reward later, and so the myth and the fact of the reality, against which these roles are played as against a backdrop, are seen in the same way as separate and distinct: myth as the means towards fact or vice versa, fact as the cause of myth or vice versa, and the ongoing struggle to perceive reality in just such a way continues even beyond the grave. Critical theories are endlessly advanced, states of permanent revolution are promulgated and the singular personality is never really given a voice.

*

The presence of Jesus:

> 'He stood at the doorpost,
> looked into the darkened room,
> knew himself to be of little consequence
> and yet looked forward eagerly to life.'

The testimony of a few lines like this is to the substance of myth as it makes its first appearance after an absence during which it certainly has not ceased to exist, but we who were left behind sorrowed for ourselves and barely knew which end of us was up.

Not that we wasted our time. We gave rational proof of our own existence by describing what little remained as the light went out. Rationally we explained reality as 'a mix of myth and fact' and we described the fallacy of undertaking a separation of one from the other, for whatever reason.

But reality is wonderful, whether we agree with it or not.

And so we may set out now to avail ourselves of myth in exemplary fashion, to deal in its substance as though it were our own and to give ourselves over to it as the various ends of time require.

For knowledge of myth is based on our immediate experience of it. We can only say that it has become flesh for our benefit, so that not to make use of that benefit would seem silly and childish. Surely the greatest vanity is to insist on poverty in the presence of riches for no other reason than that these riches are freely given and not earned or deserved by us.

Therefore let myth be seen as the gift.

If we tiptoe around it, speculating its merits and guessing its price, fearful of who will be pleased, who offended, we can make no headway. Freely out with it then, exactly as the voice of him who pronounces as he hears, who reports nothing of himself but the resources of his origin:

The first knowledge we have of myth is as strangers in our childhood. Here indeed we often enough have a hand held over our eyes as it were to make us see more clearly when we strain to overstep the boundaries set, the limits circumscribed by our genial organization.

But myth gladly enlarges upon itself. The stranger moves away, admits the restraint, and observes in astonishment how the fleeting prize out there becomes fruitful within.

Or perhaps that he desires to die in his misery. A slave to his morbid thoughts, steeped to the brow in a foreign melancholy, he lets go and leaves off, commending himself to his fate, and out there another stands up and fills his place for him.

Not that the substance of myth should depend on time. Some of us tested that often enough in our plans, our schemes for the future, our exploiting shadows cast over an ill-begotten past. We remember myth but we cannot recall it. Whyever should we recall it, when the memory of it brings it out from everywhere and links it to everything?

Myth makes its home in our heart, where fact too resides, since we cleverly conserve the innocence of our reality, and we know myth there to the extent of its greatest attraction, which it exerts over all of us who share in its knowledge and crave the possession of it. No finer birthright can ever be conceived, no more worthwhile inheritance be imagined. And yet how often do we sneak up fearfully as though someone else might steal our place at the head of the line, or we cast about among meager leavings, not properly appointed to our task at all unless appearances belie us.

How do we know myth? By the very best possible appliance of our faculties to it, faculties not as predetermined mechanisms but as developing facets of feeling, thought and imagination. We know it especially as an investment of our personal temperament, and incidentally in terms of our moods and on account of our dispositions. Sentiment allows us to strive for myth close by as though it fled in the distance, while humour struggles for it in the depths as though it reclined on high. All this is knowledge of myth. And our reality is enriched by it.

*

Knowledge of myth as riches:

We approach and become aware of our own comparative impoverishment. There is a sense of being bereft of all sense. According to this sense we continue our approach. We take care not to anticipate anything. Neither shall our sense of being bereft of all sense cling to an object or a subject. At the back of our mind rests the rational assurance we gained during the absence of the substance which now introduces itself, independent of our will and intellect, as a sense of being bereft of all sense.

This sense assures us that we face in the right direction. Remember that we seek to know myth as riches, but primarily myth as such.

Substance, as we teach in our philosophy, makes sense in the absence of subject or object and affords us a new body of knowledge. Myth as substance, in addition to making sense in this way, gives us the wherewithal to make our new body of knowledge communal. We share it with others who have this substance. This is why they are called riches, because we share them.

The communal sharing of myth as substance is an experience of wealth. This is the real wealth and those who have it require none other. Monetary or financial wealth must carry that connotation, whereas wealth in reality stands as such.

Myth as substance has this in addition to substance as such, which is first that it has a name and second that its name is Jesus. Due to it having a name it is shared in reference, and on account of its name being Jesus this reference is altogether complete.

But Jesus in all things, if we mean it as more than a doctrinal state of hopefulness and if we seek to rely on it as fact, presupposes the commitment and the equipment of our day. Only to the extent that we lay aside irrelevant concerns, mentioned in our rational beginning here as fallacies concurrent upon self-dissatisfaction and circumstantial unhappiness, can the revelation of all things as couched in myth come home to us.

Everything is mythic, and this means that we may not be left to our own devices except as rational beings from time to time, so that eternity may take hold and be come terrestrial.

One way to commit our day is by actively engaging in the pursuit of myth as riches. We intentionally lay rational structures aside and give ourselves over entirely to the incorporation of substance. Our being is held ready entirely for a human use. As soon as we make contact with substance, we search out its being as myth. Consequently we are frequently at the disposal of those who share in the same day with us, because naturally they too are preoccupied with an appreciation of substance as myth. They, like ourselves, know of no separation of work from play, of duty from ceremony, of task from performance, and so they welcome equally, along with us, an openness to everything that is mythic.

By the equipment of our day we mean the surrounding of it with thought and the perfection of it with art and all this not according to principle but in accordance with the light of day. This is our day, that it moves us to live in togetherness, and its light knows us through and through. All those things we do, to create a memorable occasion for one another and to celebrate the careful character by which our progress is made feasible, add up to the day in which we live and which properly exists for us.

The last thing to make of ourselves is a myth, because then we regret having lived to our dying day. We can make a myth of ourselves by espousing fame and fortune. But who would remind us, when the time comes, of the trouble we cause others by holding out false hope, pointing to our stature and abetting miscarriages of justice?

*

A myth and myths:

Of course we are surrounded by myths, a steady stream of them flows from the popular imagination. We may not go into the whence and wherefore of them because that would destroy us, but we may go ahead and blithely take them at face value, without adding to them or taking away from them.

That man is a rational animal, this is a myth. It means that it may be held as an opinion, adhered to as a super-stition, worked out as a philosophy, insisted upon as a religion, performed as a practical joke and so on. The hallmark of a myth is its immense versatility. We would like to say that it contains a contradiction, even a logical contradiction but this is not quite so. Neither does it marry mutually exclusives, not quite. But then the only reason why we would like to say this is that secretly we would like to be rid of myths, so that myth might reign supreme. This however is not up to us. Myths are al-lowed to restrain us, to irritate us, even to entertain us, though in this last case we have to be careful, especially careful. On the whole it will help us to keep in mind that myths will be about until the substance of myth has be-come entirely plain and clear.

What counts for us is our behaviour and conduct in the presence of myths, and in the company of those who promulgate them.

The first tenet there is to leave them be. How often af-ter all are we pressed to agree or disagree with a myth put forward under our noses? Well, it does happen, and we may be stuck for a response. Is man a rational animal? Well, is he? You there, in the third row:

'Well, yes and no.'

'What sort of an answer is that?'

'I would say that man is a rational animal when he be-haves like an animal and covers himself with a show of rationality, but man as such is difficult to get hold of in any case, because he hides behind men in reality, behind women and children at times – .'

'Charming! Is that supposed to lead to our edification?'

'Oh dear no, I was only defending my ignorance on the subject.'

'A poor defence, sir. You still stand terribly exposed.' (laughter)

Let it be. Always let them have the last word. Try to hold your end up as long as you can. Let your aim be your own true wellbeing, not your triumph over an enemy or the applause of an audience.

*

Now while it is possible to pick current myths out of the hat, or those which were current at times during the past, in Greece, Rome or China, as illustrated by artists who use them as illusions in application, it is also possible, and has been since mankind first drew breath self-consciously, to turn truths and beauties, realities in short, into myths, and to mythify them.

So for example has the life of Jesus been thoroughly mythified during the past centuries since he was killed, especially during the first fifteen or sixteen. In order to understand this, we have to distinguish between the life of Jesus and the life that is Jesus. The substance of myth as life is relevant in time, but a myth is established to create a relevance to time. So the life of Jesus, which inspires us in fact and consoles us as myth, was instead made to undergo a process of mythification, so that it

27

should rule conduct and influence behaviour. Today we can only guess at the moral issues that were involved, the skepticism that took hold of superstitious minds, the beliefs that were traded, categorized and defended, the loyalty to creeds and the sacrifice to doctrines.

The sum-total of all this mythification, even of the forces of nature and of the measures of law, has always been the world into which the child of man was born and into which he was reborn, as a child of god, though now he recognized it for what it was and had no more quarrel with it. To be in the world but not part of it was the goal of the elect, for to them being part of the world meant a stage of growth previous to their own, and the best way to serve those others was to be more intensely themselves.

This however takes us into the realm of dreams where we may abide for a time.

Here it saddens us that it should be so difficult for so many, often even for ourselves, whoever we are, to understand how a myth, myths in general, the mythic and mythification, all pertain to those things that have been left behind by us once we have discovered the ineluctable progress of mythology, the beauties and charm of myth in its various states and stages, of myth as substance, that lively and quickening principle at the heart of the universe; that point of articulation where thing is linked to thing. It saddens us because we lack patience, and our impatience is entirely justified. Yet we know ourselves to live in a dream at the moment, unfit for reality and intentionally so, on the trail of new discoveries. Our impatience is turned inward where a vast panorama of life-giving possibilities is opened up for us, bright vistas where our future may unfold itself, a future born from dream and growing gradually, by various stages of creation and contemplation, into the present, the ever-present here and now.

*

Knowledge for myth:

We awaken into a moment of aggravation and irritation. Nature, art, our own self, our work, the routines that demand our attention, all press in on us and tend to force us out of ourselves. Unpleasant sensations abound. Our nerves are in revolt. What we like to think of as our organism turns out to be as capable of chaos as the traffic in the centre of town. Hateful fires flash out from us as soon as we suspect an interruption. An interruption of what?

We are bent on the realization, for ourselves, of an eternal temperament.

This, in short, makes out our critical faculty for myth. No sense in comparing it to anything else. Temperament sleeps until circumstances awaken it. Even the world of myths and of mythification can be seen to be geared towards the rude and often brutal disturbance of our time-nature out of its self-created quietude where it declined the challenge of the world in its infancy in order all the better to rise to the critical occasion later.

My organic functions have nothing to do with any of this. No link exists between them and the external – then suddenly it stops. What has stopped? Something has stopped and has managed in this way to set up a barrier between what I can now call objective reality and my observing eye. That a barrier exists gives me something to work on; the barrier itself is imagined and used up as stuff, as raw materials.

Then a weakness sets in, an enfeeblement of the very faculty born presently out of an identifiable sensation: an interruption – a cessation. This weakness shrouds my entire being. I continue to exist, but weak. Consciousness of weakness carries me through to the next stage, which I know must come, from the fact alone of time's passing.

Because time passes whether I observe it or not, I realize that, and my weakness wins no concessions from me on account of my continuing organic existence. There exists within me a structure that cannot be broken down, and I suddenly become aware of this for the first tine. A structure for whose building and for whose upkeep I am not myself responsible. I may fully rely on it therefore in spite of weakness, interruption and cessation, and the passage of time. I may rely on this structure because it amounts to my inheritance as the single-singular human being I am. I call this structure my name, because that is what I am about.

And out of my name rises my temperament. My name is what causes the birth of my temperament, and it causes it out of itself, out of my organic, inherited structure as the person I am.

The person I am is a combination of structure and temperament, a combination of what I am about in relation to the passage of time. And time does not stop. To know this and to understand it is very valuable indeed. Not time is interrupted, not time stands still but something about myself, or better said, something I am about; something that pertains to my structural and structured organism.

That which stops has to do with humour. We might call it the life-memory, the stream of subconscious energy, but the best and most descriptive appellation for it is instinct, because it combines a definite sensitivity with a certain knowledge, and these are both absolute, or absolved. Not that material for it is lacking but that there is no material any more and that there is no material yet. This is what counts, and this makes the experience and the story of it, its history, unique. This absolute sensitivity and knowledge, like a timely deposit, rests as it were, between two ages and between the only two ages, whatever we care to call them when we point them out to each other: moments, centuries, ages – it rests between the beginning and the end of time and therefore can only be part of time itself, since time's passing remains uninterrupted.

*

However now, as I turn away from direct observation of myself, a great deal changes. My temperament, until now an object of contemplation, desires to contemplate itself, and in order to achieve this it has to step out into the light of day, where it becomes visible, in terms of awareness, tangible and concrete. Various characteristic and peculiar problems arise, because if our temperament, my temperament, is to succeed in self-contemplation, it must also make itself available to the contemplation by all human beings, and here it seems to run the risk of being faulted and wronged; it senses the danger of injustice and anticipates the pain of shame.

And yet the only way for my temperament to mature is to move into the realm of world, where it can become accessible to itself, but thereby also to human beings, including, by the way, myself as a maturing and growing human being.

The crisis of <u>my</u> temperament becoming <u>our</u> temperament can not be expressed but only acted out – or perhaps we should say that it begins by being expressed and ends by being acted out. The faculty of myth of course depends upon a genuine appreciation of this crisis, and no one can produce myth who has not himself passed through it. Those who merely approach it and shrink back do bad work, commercial in nature and popular in appeal. Their world is a realm of extinction. It lends itself to total and utter analysis. Temperament does not become self-contemplative, with the advent of world and human myth, but temper becomes self-analytical, in a world full of falsehood and lies, since it is itself a lie. Myth is not produced and absorbed, but myths are manufactured, idolized, argued about and destroyed. Instead of mythology being the communal function of human beings who seek to love one another, there is an ongoing mythification of people by people, of population in extinction by minds in dissolution, of the world by the ego. Upon the most thorough-going and final analysis of this mythification of the world by the ego, we have nothing but an infinite number of points of resistance against reality and points of flight from reality – and that might be the best way of putting it at the moment.

But let us turn away from this exercise in futility and return to our critical appreciation of temperament for myth.

*

Temperament for myth:

Here we have to do with temperament in self-contemplation as the common stock of mythic humanity.

It stands to reason that where human beings live in society and communicate in fellowship, they treasure the memory of their past and cherish their plans for a future, and this is where myth in particular comes in because it makes this possible. We might call myth the shape of things past and of things to come, and due to this shape these things of another time are of use to us presently.

In the absence of myth, or where myth substance is neglected, the past becomes a self-concealing trap and the future takes on an other-worldly appearance with an unhealthy lure about it or a feeling of dread, while the present boils down to material mechanisms.

Temperament in self-contemplation, the one we are justified in calling 'our' temperament, creates myth and makes it available. It does this by consciously drawing on instinct in the presence of world. The presence of world is of critical importance. Remember that world initially rises out of my temperament in crisis. World consequently is myth in substance related to itself and seen, or understood, as a whole, in completeness; world is finished, and therefore endless,

So the presence of world during the creation of myth is important because it lends measure, dimension and extension, to what would otherwise come to an introverted, improbable end. Our temperament measures itself against world just as my own temperament, prior to its crisis, when world was still a hopeful state in the future for it or a lost paradise in the past, took the measure of whatever it contacted, weighed and appraised it, and compared it to itself and to its effects.

My own temperament of course was not capable of producing myth. It could only push here, pull there, twist elsewhere, to find out what would happen, but always secretly aware of a special and unique possibility holding within itself the foreshadowing of an exquisite experience due to an achievement of sorts. This knowledge was built into my temperament and it was mentioned earlier. How did it get there? Instinctively. And instinct works by heredity. Did man have a beginning? It might be interesting to suppose so. When did the first human being live? When and where? Less interesting, because it makes myth depend strangely on fact, to the detriment of both. Do we think differently today? It depends on who we are.

But all my inherited organization, the way I am put together and the way I work, how my parts fit in such a way that what I said just now came out in that particular fashion : all this is derived through instinct and it exists blindly until I become aware of it, and then I marvel and call it Christ. 'A definite sensitivity combined with a certain knowledge, both absolute and absolved,' was how we described it earlier, in a moment of myth. We blithely talk about 'the human race', 'mankind', 'human beings', but not quite as frequently do we mention how the human race is fashioned as a unique thing, organically constructed, so that one thing or another may work itself out, may slide into a central position, join up with whatever has stood ready for it; how mankind as such, too, may be viewed as the marvellous building it represents, func-

34

tional thought coming to its pitch, opportunities taken by forces long ready and waiting, an intelligence for centuries carried unconsciously, a dream-burden in blood forwarded until circumstances have grown decisive, then suddenly glowing out, casting shadows where previously nothing stood to interrupt no light.

And where this central efficiency of human endeavour gradually found itself guessed at – well, it had to happen somewhere – absolute and absolved, always between ages, before time and after time, there it was eventually recognized by a few well-sighted personages who had nothing better to do than to concern themselves with such a thing, and they knew it to be on the move, soon to flash out, to be endowed with personality and a name, to grow as high up as that, if you like, into such a stratosphere of specialization and complexity as personality and name at a date, some place. They called him the anointed One. There were men, and there was man, but finally, difficult to take in because so starkly simple and easy, there was the man. The man was on the cards, for a few, long before he had fully evolved and chosen a face. The human race gradually filtered out manhood, if you like, and then mankind delivered up the man, the anointed One, we know where – it had to be somewhere. Why quarrel with dates and places? Why take arrogant pride in what could not have been helped and then lose it all for a time anyway, just to show that it has nothing to do with vanity and perfect externals.

The absolute, inherited instinct becomes mythic substance.

Jesus Christ was born.

Myth and fact, both real. Both the same reality. Each describes what the other states. If we have one we have them both. Facts have a history, while myth makes history.

*

Myth makes history:

When craziness surrounds me where I tender
affections fond but none accept my peace,
I turn to this last hope: my soul's defender
and here cry out, that pain and torture cease.

Outside a blackbird makes the evening sing
so cool and calm, I long that it may heal me.
Oh fresh green boughs of billowing lime in spring,
I pray that your white light may not conceal me.

For everywhere I look the sun has masked
the walls with glow, the clouds with metal shining,
These things support me, but my god has asked
that I be dumb and to his death inclining.

One day, this, only one day out of many
and my life stops, as though I had not any.

*

Bitter reproach surrounds my every move
and dull constraint upheaves my inner being.
My unguarded eye would charge, my tongue reprove,
though willed, I cease from hearing as from seeing.

Keep fit for me my flesh till I return
and make no use of spirit without flavour.
In heat let love freeze, hate in order churn
to heart's content, but taste this poison savour.

All sanctions have dispelled the laws that prosper
merely by force, though violence still makes hay.
Spirit makes gain – the fetish heartthrob's loss per
annum runs high : it woos and wastes away.

The night stalks quietly, long streets mark its going,
while some men harvest: reaping, storing – sowing.

*

Myth makes history because it influences our way of
doing things. The decisions we make ourselves.

If we refuse to decide, there is no way for myth to
come into our doing and consequently it accumulates
upon our being and crushes us.

The depression of moods is like this. Religious decision, central to our being as its unique expression of itself, such as the decision to accept our child or to restore
our spouse, either from the start or upon a 'death of love',
lifts the depression of moods and surely makes us susceptible of myth. But of course since the substance of myth
is personal, we cannot expect to coerce it. What we can
coerce however is our own indecisive self. It stands for
indecision. It cannot make choices but it merely reacts,
Neither can I move from my self by a chain of events to a
world of reality, since mere reaction excludes and prevents myth. It is precisely such an impossible chain we
imagine when we wish to justify our selves when we
ought to consider freeing ourselves. Then again, we ought
not, but we may.

A self accumulates due to the pressure of myth not
recognized. An ego is built up and structured as a result
of myth refused. The existence of a self and of an ego can

37

usually be taken for granted in all but the gods, and one soon learns through bitter experience how an insistence on a state of knowledge and accomplishment soon reveals ignorance and failure.

In time, then, myth is refused by us and we fail to recognize it, it might be most expedient to admit it in a modest and a humble spirit, in which great knowledge is gained. What matters is what we do then.

History begins out of a modest recognition of our ego and it starts in a humble acceptance of our self. Better said, it starts as soon as I accept that I have a self, that I have failed to recognize myth, somewhere along the line, it matters little where, and begins out of my recognition of the fact that I have an ego, that I have refused myth here or there. As soon as I accept this, freely and openly, no matter who wants to know, my ego lies available in front of me, subject to reason, and my self stands open to the influence of love.

Reason and love, mythically derived, make for form and content of history to the extent of my ego and as far as my self goes, and here we view these negative principles as raw material and as stuff input, awkward as that sounds. Once my self is fully invested and my ego efficiently used up, history, until now as form and content, begins to take shape. Love and reason are not any longer distinguishable, and we should mention that until the advent of history as shape, reason and love were in fact distinguishable, as functions of the past, though in no way separable. Now that history is fully in progress, and while it is in progress, there can be no question of ego or self, of mine or yours, but only of our willingness towards myth, which in retrospect we would have to call our willingness towards more myth, recalling that history began, even the history of mankind, due to myth and to our acceptance of the fact that we failed to recognize it and that we refused it.

So when we say that myth makes history, we imply liberation and freedom : liberation from self and ego and then freedom in world. The purpose of history is liberation from self and ego, and freedom in world is its end.

History could therefore be called the structure of myth, because that is what myth is about : the working out of events in their effects on us and then the working out of ourselves in our effects on each other. Progress should always be measured in terms of: from the personal to the communal. Such is the progress of history. We may regard it in the small or in the large.

Out of the cooperation of an individual human being with myth arise our greatest historical successes and triumphs. There can be no greater historical success than your individual liberty achieved, and no greater historical triumph is possible than personal freedom attained in world.

While myth makes history, an individual human being, like myself or you, either takes advantage of this or stumbles and falls. Whether one or the other depends on our choice at a certain moment.

To take advantage of the historicity of myth, of the history that is to be made by myth, means first of all to welcome a fact of myth, which is to say that myth is around here and now in a certain instance or given case, and then, as growing immediately out of such a welcome, it is the organic absorption of the mythic effects. Criticism would, and often sadly does, curtail the welcome by denying myth its factuality and so making a myth out of it, which is a falsehood, and so the food is pushed away and cannot be eaten. Where a welcome has successfully been extended, in spite of criticism, we are still not home free, because the mythic effects, instead of being absorbed, can still be forestalled and prevented, as they often tragically are, by extinct and professional science, so that they are listed, categorized, compartmentalized, counted and 'data processed' in the fond hope of an eventual opinion to be formed, conclusion to be drawn or judgment to be made, which of course can never happen.

A certain instance of myth is welcome insofar as we give ourselves over to rational thought on the occasion of an experience of our own nature. I may for example decide to deprive myself of an indulgence in some pleasure for no other reason than that the boredom usually visited on sensual self-sufficiency strikes me as an evil greater than the good to be derived from the pleasure. The experience of our own nature here, couched innocently enough in terms of a moral reminiscence, is governed and made to abide by a principle of order. I may be a student who struck his teacher with his fist because that same teacher struck him as an evil-minded bully with a flair for sarcastic slights aimed at dispassionate young females all demure in the front row. A quick apology and the frank admission that I was wrong to behave in this way do not deprive me of the benefits I gained by acting as I did, but they do save me from the boring harangues of a disciplinary committee and from that dreadful feeling of being perfectly and pointlessly right, not to mention publicly justified.

That the sensual self-sufficiency of an insistence on private right should be weighed in the rational balance against personal integrity and a public disclaimer, amounts to the welcome of a certain instance of myth. It has to occur to me to think like this, and no amount of derivative cogitation dependent upon self-serving impulses and reflecting to any degree on an ego in fight or flight can discover such a line of thought for me – indeed it would obscure the very possibility of it. Then, when in fact I do think like this, I extend the welcome to the occurrence. Of course I still have to make the critical decision, in favour of the disclaimer and my integrity, casting face-saving tactics to the winds, before I can act accordingly and then organically absorb the ensuing effects.

Having documented a certain instance of myth up to the initial point of organic absorption, we can do the same now for a given case of myth.

Assume you walk along a country road until you come to a gate through which you enter. A path leads between meadows past whitethorn bushes fresh in bloom. A stand of majestic beeches and spreading sycamore rises up the hillside to your right, on the left some long stretches of sandstone wall surround a plot of meadow and fruit trees. Then onward, up a slight incline, and near the middle of a sheltered place surrounded by tall trees and high bushes, stand three rough tables with benches. You sit down, rest and look about you. You decide to write a few lines of poetry but you limit yourself almost entirely to the effects that appeal to you from that realm which you have become accustomed to calling the light of day and which you might define as the presence of a human being on earth. Given that you are a human being, you will document your presence, for a time, on the earth, and this presence will be a given case of myth. You will have to wait for it until it suits you and you will make yourself as suitable as possible. The outcome goes as follows:

> Oh let me say these walls of crooked stone
> and ponds of bluebells in among the beeches!
> The blossom-down from rhododendron lies
> on sun-spilled paths. Three dancing cabbage whites
> sow light beneath great overhanging boughs
> of candled chestnut. Yellow poppies glow
> some yards away. A freckled daisy patch
> now gleams and glistens while my eye endures.

> A cypress strains, contorts towards the sky,
> no alien sky, but one so full of rich blue
> that wisps of white cloud melt before its gaze.
> Oh god, up there lies such a prize of joy
> that hoverflies hold stillest in mid air
> to concentrate a speck of atmosphere
> and then dash on. A fluttering blackbird makes
> mock hay among the litter of dry leaves.

While you wrote these lines of poetry you were aware of the need to wait for myth to be given, one detail at a time, until the entire case of myth was entailed. But you also realized that there was something you had to do within yourself which would continue to make room, as it were, for more details of myth until the entire case of myth had been received.

And here we come face to face again with the communal aspect of our more mature activity, because while you absorbed psychosomatically, within yourself, the effects of myth, you also wrote words down. It would have been impossible to do one without the other. Had you written nothing down, the absorption would have been merely somatic, skin-deep, effective for a while only, and had you not involved yourself organically with what was happening you might have jotted down a few notes, a literal impression or two, and that would have been that.

One important thing to remember here is that while the organic absorption and the verbal record cannot go on independently from one another, since both are required for myth to make history, nevertheless the record remains as an opportunity, a possibility and an offering, a poem on paper, as readily destroyed, one supposes, as anything else on paper, while the operation of instinct stores up riches that are permanent and last. What you have gained, in other words, not due to writing lines of poetry on paper, nor due to the poetic process within you, technically, but due to available myth welcomed and absorbed, is a deposit of reality; and more, an increase of humanity, which on one hand cannot be taken away or destroyed and on the other hand contributes to your next piece of work, which might this time be spoken rather than written, or manually performed.

So when we say that myth makes history, we do well to keep in mind that the substance of myth is personal and graciously given, that it may be seen as a universal performance or conceived as a cosmic trend, but finally what is required is a single human being, an individual person, you or I, and unless I am willing to become mythic myself, I can in no way participate in the community of human beings, which participation is the greatest good, but I remain critical, disenchanted outside, disappointed away from home; I might even fabricate a world of my own out of bitterness and self-reproach, out of legality and historic necessity, out of criticism and a future plan, out of moral indignation and social commitment – the number of accidents is endless, but eventually all such worlds disintegrate under the cumulative pressures of contemporary existence or in the face of as little as a single example of myth in the flesh.

*

Myth in the flesh:

Flesh is whatever seems to exist but it does not.

Myth always exists, but this is not everywhere apparent.

So myth in the flesh is really a contemplative entity and not to be reached with the intellect alone or achieved with the will alone. On the other hand, it has nothing to do with clear vision or pure dream and should not be confused with them,

'Unique' and 'peculiar' are adjectives well suited to describe it. Whether we wish to get at it directly or discuss aspects of it, there is always the feeling of being not quite in touch or the suspicion that we may have missed the point. One difficulty seems to lie in our inability to apply an appropriate concept. Nor can our imagination, even when coaxed to do its utmost, arrive at a satisfactory piece of knowledge about what interests here. We are dealing with something unique which has no uniqueness, and though it strikes us as peculiar, we cannot for the life of us put our finger on its peculiarity.

Myth in the flesh is the example; not an example of this or that, but simply and solely the example. This is the way it's done and this is the way it is, there are no explanations. The example springs to mind. We do with it what we want and make of it what we like.

The example is available because of something that has been done in the past. The succession of events keeps us in touch with it. Tradition creates the bounds for it.

The example is available in order to make something possible in the present, right here and now and in the light of day. What it does make possible is live and can only be lived. Due to the availability of the example we may live wholly and completely.

In order to avail ourselves of the advantages that incur upon knowledge of the example, we need no historic background to the cause of it, although it helps. We need only an immediate knowledge of what it is that gives itself in the exemplary fashion.

So we can divide our task in two here and concern ourselves, first and quite independently from past causes, with myth in the flesh as the example available to our immediate knowledge right here and now and in the light of day, and then, if we like, we can undertake a separate inquiry into what it was that was done in the past that created the example and along with it its eventual tradition through the intervening days, times and ages. The concept of generation will stand us in good stead there. A power is generated in the past due to the Life acted out and we today benefit. This is easy enough to say but really quite marvellous.

But first we intend to know the example today, and today, by the way, means right here and now and in the light of day, and it takes less time to write down; not that time saved is everything.

To know the example means to set an example; we led up to this in the previous section on myth making history. In other words as we become familiar with it, we also act it out. Sometimes we act surprised, when this happens rather than being done by us. One interprets it as a debility of self-consciousness. Although such an interpretation would be wrong if it contained a criticism, it can be avoided if we take care to do consciously what would otherwise have to happen, unconsciously.

Knowledge of the example can begin from an instinct for the society of human beings, which is a reality, and not to be confused with the society of man, which is an idea, or the society of people, which is an ideal. Ideal society is more of a burden than anything else and it stems from a rejection of real or human society,[1] and idealism in any of this becomes a downright curse, thriving on abstractions.

An instinct for the society of human beings promises to enrich us with an increase of knowledge of ourselves, and we learn from experience that such knowledge can only be gained in that society and not immediately or directly of ourselves. So consequently we seek out human

---

[1] Human society – always towards community.

beings. And there too we can make the mistake of seeking knowledge of ourselves through them rather than in their society.

But the society of human beings can only make sense to us and be effective for us once it includes ourselves. The bare intellect is left behind and the will as such is cast out. The key to human society is not either one or the other. What remains is our willingness to be accepted in good faith and on trust.

This particular trust has to be developed, by us, in ourselves. Of course it is always there, however whether or not we know where it is and can make use of it at the appropriate moment depends on habits of trust acquired and on skills of good faith worked out. Trust as a habit or skill is no ordinary common or garden accomplishment. We build it up in adversity, become resilient in holding it out to those we find ourselves mistrusting, become imaginative in extending it into areas of new experience, magnanimous in returning it where we discover that previously we have withdrawn it. In trust we have a weapon, a tool and an instrument. It supplies us with the one unfailing basis for all our deeds, and where it holds, nothing we do can go wrong,

We can also build up our trust violently. This simply means that we trust that we trust. It works as an exercise or as a special effect. Such special effects cannot be discounted. We can also love that we love, which trains our love violently, again either as an ability or a power of special effect. If anyone thinks such violence is pointless, let him look around him. There is a time and a place for violence. Here it works in our favour, and not least by discountenancing violence there.

The main thing, as things go, about real violence, which is violence in the spirit, as compared to violence then and there, which is violence in the flesh, is that it cures the flesh and renders it whole, and since we mean the flesh as such, this, naturally, includes our own, by involving it, drawing it into the process of growth.

More specifically now, spiritual growth of a violent nature inculcates brain. This may take time to understand, and calling to mind that live science establishes its own current limitations will gain us patience.

Brain substance generally records and correlates everything. We move in the realm of comparative mathematics now and a discipline of a high order is required. Considering the nature of substance, if brain substance generally records and correlates everything, then it goes without saying that brain substance is in general a record and a correlation of everything. An inculcation of brain therefore may be fairly described as a creation of brain substance, rendering it particular.

Imagine a computer that contains all possible data of information. It stores everything, but as a possibility. You come along and you want something, not everything, but in actuality, so you appeal to the machine in a certain way. What the machine then does for you is an analogy for an inculcation of brain. The extinct brain is of course itself very much like a computer, insofar as it stores information and gives it up on command, not even actualizing it like our imagined computer, and those who prefer to think of their brain in that way only increase their hold on their own extinction. *Mais chacun à son goût.*

One is tempted to ask: the inculcation of brain on what? in the same way as one would like to ask: the abstraction of life from what? whenever the physical meaning of such terms becomes more relevant? However the response would always have to be couched in other terms, for the simple reason that there is more to reality than the physical or the mental, than the process or the state, than growth or diminishment. Even if we were to suggest that an inculcation 'of' the brain plays more or less over into (the area of meaning opened out by) an inculcation 'by' the brain, we would still struggle with the same problem, though on another plane. It remains therefore for each one of us to get as far as he can with these contemplative entities and where possible we may even improve on our intuitive grasp.

It should also be added, as a caution, that the exercise of trust violently and the training of love violently, this contemporary ascesis, cannot be managed by me by myself or by you by yourself, in monkish seclusion or isolated hermetically in an individual mind or body, but it can only be done by us, today, in awareness of each other, as a social activity in the beautiful sense of the word. It can in fact even help us, this ascetic activity, in the discovery and prolongation of such a beautiful sense of the word, whereupon we may gain an aesthetic sense, which is never the specialty of a private individual but always a communal amplitude and as such the very stuff of what we mean by society (towards community).

*

49

This brings us to the end of our inquiry into the example and we can now undertake, with industry, a similar but quite independent inquiry into that which was done in the past to make the example today possible.

The main problem here will always be one of a collective or folk memory. On one hand we hope that one thing happened, because that would justify and at least partly explain our fears, while on the other hand we act from a certainty about the past, an automatic, instilled and ingrained posture that takes us aback at times while demanding to be taken for granted.

A well-reasoned argument can do nothing for us. The past is not derived from the present any more than the future is derived from the past. The only question that really needs to be asked is: How can anything that is done in the past have such an effect that today we may draw on it and be influenced by it without any direct or even indirect reference to it? How can it be 'in the flesh' for us, in other words, not just recalled in mind or passed on by word of mouth or letter?

We maintain, first of all, that there is such a thing as myth in the flesh, and we have demonstrated how it works, (this alone would suffice to encourage anyone who still wants courage as to the viability and validity of this – whatever it is. I do not really mind what you call it, some say, as long as I can make use of it, and this betokens a nice, practical wisdom. Why quibble about labels once you are happy with the contents of the jar?

And the same practical sense demands: So what can it gain me to disturb myself about the past or about anything that happened then, when I can obviously get all I need in terms of spiritual sustenance from present day world?

The answer of course is that it can gain me nothing, but it can gain us everything, This with respect to why one should bother. Such entities as family, community, society and world have one thing in common that makes them relevant and valuable, and that is my willingness, or your willingness, to suffer for us.

The social impulse of course is strong enough in most individuals to carry them once or twice across the boundaries of an inner isolation or an outward privacy; the problem with impulses however is that while they start a process going, once or a number of times, they will not and cannot keep it up. They put us into the notion but they cannot keep us up to the mark – where we need to be, at least for a time, if the process is to take on a momentum of its own. A dynamic of living does not happen but it is brought about, and without such a steady willfulness of all our best – of all my or your best – faculties, abilities and skills, not to mention gifts and talents, I continue to fall back into my self, you back into your self, and none of our communications really prosper.

I in my self and you in your self are lost, this is what it means to be lost. An individual becomes the individual. A particular organism embodies particularity.

But of course the communal impulse can be followed up, the social spark may be blown into flame. This means first of all that I have to stop picturing myself as out there somewhere.

When I fall in love, it doesn't need to stop there. I can go on and love.

Once I have learned to love and have made a good habit of doing it, which habit is all that counts when it comes, finally, to exploiting an impulse and capitalizing on it, it makes no sense for me to 'want to fall in love again', as it were. The habit of loving has put me in touch with you on a permanent basis and we can now with right speak in terms of ourselves. Naturally, no matter how much you love me, I still remain free to return to my self, my individuality as such, to my insistence on my rights and privileges as a liberal agent, unattached to your inter-fering influences and not bound by your domineering be-haviour, your … etc. The same goes for you. Nothing I do can make you continue with me on a familiar basis and in social harmony.

Once I realize, however, how much is to be gained for me by remaining in touch with you instead of falling back or allowing myself to be pushed back, by laziness, say, or my own foul temper – into a previous state rather than going on to the next venture – I naturally want to do something if at all possible to make it less likely for me to make a fool of myself in the future – I say *naturally* because the way I am when we are together makes much more sense to me than the way I am when I insist on my independence from you and on my self-sufficiency in my self. Within the context of a science one can differentiate between my self, to which I do not wish to return because it excludes us, and myself, which I can only be along with you and while I welcome your presence.

So in order to continue to be myself and avoid becoming my self I have to work and be for us, and the only way I can directly or indirectly work and be for us is by showing how this myth in the flesh today is due to a certain act in the past and by identifying this act, demonstrating how it was performed, describing what I know of it – in short by remembering it.

And of course we cannot get around it that the act had to be performed by someone – since acts do not perform themselves, in comparison to events, which come about, and to accidents, that happen – and that this someone lived and had a name. Often I try to get around it, for some strange reason. It is as though I were ashamed of thinking of that person and of mentioning that person's name, so that I talk around the topic, and I go to some lengths to posit forces and assume laws where a particular person was concerned; or I institute relations and suggest analogies where that particular person really had a name. Not that there is anything shameful in itself about being a person or having a name; I am a person with a name myself and – not ashamed of that, surely. Or I explain the wish to avoid that person and to avoid mentioning that name by the fact that for so long in the past, right up to the near present, so much has been perpetrated and justified allegedly in the name of that person which strikes me today as doubtful and ambivalent and arbitrary that I would rather keep clear of the whole business than incur an ugly squabble or arouse disgraceful feelings by – 'becoming personal and mentioning names'.

Though much of what has been done in the past right up to the near present, allegedly in the name of that person, has left me free to be myself, even while stupidly setting out to destroy my self and perhaps even succeeding in doing so, time and again. For it occurs to me today that all the powers in the world cannot destroy me and all the forces of evil combined can only destroy my self and never me, and where it was imagined that the destruction of my self would in any way lead directly or indirectly to my birth as a real person, a human being with a name, there a mistake was being made. Though where I insist on my self I thank Christ I am cut off and where I complain of this may my mouth be stopped,

Better by far however to leave our selves be and concentrate on the memory of what has made us possible, and through us myself and yourself.

It would seem worth repeating, that something is definitely available today through the use of which, although it bears neither title nor office nor even a name – nor can it, as far as that goes, be conceptualized or stated – through the instinctive employment of which, I say, we may achieve the society of human beings, the community of kindred spirits and the vision and habitat of world – something I have called myth in the flesh and I described it as such. This does not suffice in itself if we want to establish ourselves on a permanent basis and to minimize, perhaps to prevent entirely, a periodic return to extinction and to a structured self. In order to succeed where we have arrived we must actually work to remember the source and cause of this myth in the flesh and the act that brought it into reality. Only when I work directly for us and indirectly for myself will there be no room for my self and neither time nor energy for me to return to it or to construct one.

Memory and identification then are required to advance the work and sink the foundations of human society.

That the recalling of recorded facts is not what we mean by memory here should hardly need to be mentioned. On the other hand we wish to be bound by facts, because of our definite interest in the actual past, which has nothing to do with fantasy and mental invention.

Now the actual past rings true as a concept, but also it clatters, and this as soon as we allow it to empty itself of its human content.

That the actual past we study remain human depends on us who make the inquiry. To this end we identify, so that whatever comes before our eyes is subjected to a selection procedure, becoming, consequently, during the interval, objective.

Whatever we subject to our influence becomes, during the interval, objective – this again goes without saying, but what must be said, and repeated often in the present time, is that whatever is subjected to human influence reveals its humanity. This objective humanity interests us.

The objection that a human inquiry must naturally constitute a bias in favour of a specifically human interest and that such a bias must prejudice reality, reveals an utter ignorance as to humanity and human beings and must be rejected as an absurdity and as criticism. Reality must be protected carefully against realism, in this case against the misguided notion of humanity as an accident, equivalent to primates, vegetation and sea water. Equally the criticism that we make use of what we have in order to plumb the source of it must be met with : Of course! Naturally! How else could it be, again considering who we are and what we are dealing with?

Normally therefore it should suffice to speak of our past or of the human past, which is the past subjected to a process of selection by a human being and so rendered momentarily objective, (or temporarily objective, depending on whether we identify inwardly, aiming to achieve a universal relevance, or outwardly, in consideration of cosmic wholeness), but in the face of criticism, whether it arises within ourselves or elsewhere, we would speak of the human past as ordained and we would specify ordination as an aspect of the identification process. And against this ordained past we would have to set the unordained, or ordinary past, to which selection would generally be misapplied, or else one picks around in it for a bit of historical consolation.

Insofar as we identify various constituents of the past as we see it, we must rid ourselves, for the sake of the task in hand, of every last shred of self-consciousness in the interest of optimal awareness, by which we mean the greatest degree of awareness that is favourable or advantageous, leaving room for an intentional or voluntary ignorance of what we sense to be out of order or beyond the pale of the past that interests us; we do not eradicate self-conscious impulses or deaden ourselves to them, but we view them with respect, which would be self-respect, and then we revise them and invest them in awareness: this is called a critique of the past, and if there is time we propose to discuss it at length, as an important aspect of history and of the writing of history which is sometimes deprecated and frequently misunderstood, Also the concept of optimal awareness, as against maximum awareness, would merit a thorough investigation, along with its sister concept of pragmatic ignorance, where we come to realize that one can in some cases be over-aware, hypersensitive to all impulses and emotionally strung out, at the expense of our organic equilibrium and our spiritual soundness, implying fanatic zeal and a sacrificial temperament. Sacrifice in any case is to be deplored in these matters, and since it constitutes probably the most popular and widespread of all doomed views of the past, we do well to emphasize now and again the merciful essence of optimal awareness – in order to shake off a negative we must espouse a positive – and of any truly just critique.

The selection procedure which renders the past human, and makes it our past, implies a set of remembered data and involves a series of memorable events.

Memorable events, as part of the past, are given and they occur, and we know them by this, by the fact that they are given and that they occur. We do not have to search them out or to construe them, from among imaginary material or out of a controlled supply of traditional stuff. Taken one at a time, at face value, they develop into a series, and such a series illustrates a period of memory,

Remembered data take time to accumulate and we assimilate them as part of our temperament. As such we might as well describe them as moments of past time. Their appearance in terms of anything other than more past time, as remembered data, cannot be ascertained and so we wait for a set of them to accumulate. This happens gradually. But we assimilate such a set of them abruptly. An analogy of this is the act of chewing and swallowing, where the former takes time to accumulate and the latter abruptly takes place, in this case in the stomach, but there as temper.

Remembered data as temper compare to memorable events as moods.

Distinguish between temper and a temper. Also between moods and a mood. They vastly differ.

Temper refers the past, or past time, to the present, or to present time, so that whatever occurs to us as past reality becomes contemporary. This is important. We say that the past must be tempered and that it must become contemporary before it can be properly experienced.

So we have access to the whole past and to everything that is past, but only while our memory is well tempered. To an ill-tempered memory the past discloses itself only partially and there can be no excellence, nothing masterful. This is so and it falls out like this precisely because we then take some aspect of the past for the whole past and bring all our organs of experience to bear on it.

One has become accustomed to speaking of memory, and of one's memory, as though it were an organ, but the organ is our temperament, and in terms of it we function and apply ourselves in memorable fashion. In order to keep in touch, clearly and sanely, with our past, we must see to our temperament, as a faculty and as a skill, because here we can directly or indirectly prove and improve

– so that in turn, then, our temper will be clarified and our memory, our remembering, will become effective.

The best way to create temperament is by overcoming our likes and dislikes. This does not mean that we turn against them but rather that we become conscious of them as sensible equivalents. If something puts us off, we take care not to be put off by it. This creates temperament If something turns us on we take care not to be turned on by it. This also creates temperament. But be careful about how you judge here. When you take care not to be put off by whatever it is that puts you off, you do not reject the thing but you neutralize the accidental effect it has on you, which does not negate or kill the effect but strips it of its prejudicial character so that meaning and purpose may shine through. The same thing goes for when you refuse to be turned on by something.

The popular thing of course is to give in to what turns us on and to reject what puts us off. Consequently popularity has neither purpose nor meaning but it deflates our energy and fatigues our strength. While behaving in a popular fashion we can neither grow nor thrive, but we become extinct and die, possibly in front of the applauding masses.

Now this is one thing, to accept and reject what we like and dislike, what turns us on and puts us off, so that we decline and diminish, eventually to be extinguished, snuffed out by time as it were, not to be remembered but famous or infamous, depending on whether our popularity pleased or displeased the crowds assembled in churches, schoolrooms and concert halls. To the extent of our popularity, which is self-gained renown, we must be purged and cleansed in the end.

However quite another thing is to discover that our likes and dislikes dissipate and mislead, and then to react, even vengefully, first by attempting to dissociate ourselves from all things that affect us positively or negatively, even going so far as to destroy what pleases or displeases us, or, when we are forced to admit that the number of such things is infinite and that we no sooner get rid of one but another three crop up, we turn against ourselves and kill off the sensitive being. We do not become extinct and die now but we are in fact and in truth extinct and dead. With a little bit of effort, continuously applied, that state of extinction and death can be perpetuated quite successfully – but this is horrible. While behaviour in accordance with our likes and dislikes was a tragic error, this willful destruction of our sensitive selves, this physical exit from life, is a damnable mistake.

So surely we must be getting some insight now into the difference between, on one hand, not allowing ourselves to be put off by what puts us off and on the other hand putting off what puts us off or getting rid of ourselves; between on one hand not allowing ourselves to be turned on by what turns us on and on the other hand turning on the thing that turns us on or negating it and ultimately, again, getting rid of our-selves.

Also, we overcome our likes and dislikes again and again, and we look forward to being given opportunities to do so because we do after all want our temperament to improve, to increase in resilience, to become capable of more vigorous and more sensitive responses.

Mainly, so far, we have spoken about the creation of temperament, by which the most apathetic nature may divest itself of its apathy and gain some fibre, some grain and some grit. We have actually spent more time discussing what not to do and what an overcoming of our likes and dislikes does not mean, but this seems appropriate to our day,

Keeping in mind now that liking and disliking are doing something, or that they are something specific – not the same as being fond of something, finding something distasteful, though in the same category as these – indeed with all those expressed sensations that we *find*, one way or another, finding them odd, difficult, etc., we can now go on to describe how temperament, once created, can and should right away be invested, because without this it only disintegrates and has to be started up again from scratch, as witness the behaviour of a temperamental nature, where likes and dislikes are overcome, only to be replaced by stronger ones to which one gives in.

We can study the investment of temperament as temper. When we try this and fail, and make a bad habit of such failure, we gain a reputation for having a temper, and what we do not have is temper. So how exactly can we go about it when we mean to succeed?

Patience is the essence; patience and the downright will to succeed. After all we are not the first to attempt it. More is involved than the sustaining of an equilibrium, a balance of power. An actual problem is required against which we can pit our acquired temperament, and this problem must be large enough, complicated enough, obscure enough, to challenge the faculty and skill in our possession.

Now we find that problems are generally tailor-made to fit the requirements of the temperament that comes up against them, but this can only be really so in every instance where one trusts in the justness and fitness of one's personal circumstance. So it is no good preaching optimism or pessimism, as we do hypocritically, but we need to teach trust. Just as it takes a specific approach to the past to render it and to reveal its humanity, so does it take intimate trust to discover how the problems we meet are just the right size. And, to repeat, an insistence on the actual world being the best of all possible worlds does no good at all and only depresses us or seduces us to ridicule unless we first learn and teach by example to put our trust in trust. No good trusting my self; that is not trustworthy. However there is such a thing as trust which can be trusted, and it can also be trusted to gain us a clear view of our problems as proportionate to our needs when it comes to the investment of temperament as temper.

Two problems face us even now: Where do we find trust, so that we may trust it, in this all too familiar of faithless generations, and what do we do with our problem, how do we solve it, once we know for a certainty that it suits us to the ground?

Trust is found wherever a lack of trust is opposed. We overcome our likes and dislikes, our found life, by pulling the rug out from under it and flying away on it as a temperament carpet, and now we oppose, as we overcame then, but this time our lack of trust, our distrust, mistrust, even suspicion, lends itself to it; and of course we do not have to stop at our own lack of trust, as we come across it again and again in ourselves and in our actions, available there to afford us an opportunity, but we may equally oppose mistrust in others insofar as it affects us, which it invariably seems to do.

We will not here discuss the organic and biological implications of a lack of trust and the extent to which a morbid or critical passivity contains germinally the energy required for trust from the start, because we are much more interested in the application of trust more and more automatically, so that a lack of trust, in one and the same person, is exploited nearly as a reflex, curing the flesh incidentally.

Now that we may trust our circumstances and realize that the problem, as a circumstance, suits us, we may begin to generate the energy that will turn the problem into an issue, which means that anyone who cares to understand the problem can help us with it and we in turn, whether we get help or not, may deal with it in reference to established fact. While the problem still pertains to me in the singular, the way all problems that are worth their salt arise, I cannot be helped, that goes without saying, but also I can do nothing with it, analytically or critically. So we might say that the first step towards the investment of temperament as temper, unless we count the compilation of trust, is a generation of organic energy in order to make an issue of the problem where primarily we may see it in perspective and secondarily we may be helped.

Temperament has now become socially acceptable. Up to now we may have found that our peers have rejected us and that other human beings have been making social allowances for us, in terms of suffering, tolerance and actual discipline. Due to our own commitment to the problem – due to my commitment to my problem – I have shown that I mean business, and this attracts interest. Of course I mustn't count on that interest or try to create it by influencing others directly.

And a human being's first and main problem always turns out to be the perception of time. Sooner or later I have to pit myself against that, and then I think of it not so much as yet another one among many, but as <u>the</u> problem, and when this one is solved, all the rest will be child's play. So it would seem that the sooner a person gets around to the main problem the better, especially at the time of youth when strength is best. That time is perceived, time – not the time – it all comes down to that, and how we eventually end up managing it differs of course from one person to the next; but that we manage it, this gives us everything in common.

So time is the thing that each one of us sees but each one in his or her own way, Happily there can be no seeing it the same. Joyfully there can be no hearing it the same, Your contact with it cannot be mine and that makes us both glad . The singular personality is a unique perception of time. Or conversely, there can be no more than one perception of time at a time. I could go on for hours explaining to you what time is and you would take pleasure from my version of time, and the pleasure would join us but your own version of time would be quite otherwise.

And so with each child of man on earth.

And yet, while we keep our faculties applied to time itself we cannot achieve greatness. We can give one another pleasure, we can be happy together and we can joyfully share each other's company, and this is much. But more is possible.

Consequently the disturbance in the garden. Consequently the unrest in the park.

More is possible, so the snake whispers its temptation; the hero throws down his challenge, the heretic makes his protest.

Why should more be possible? We are all such a happy family, with our vision of ourselves as the chosen people, with our monopoly on civilization, our exclusive right to the social favour of God. Let us kill these prophets, neglect these heroes, excommunicate these heretics. They disturb us in our vision of ourselves as perfect and complete, they irritate our notion of ourselves as the champions of the downtrodden, as the upholders of the faith, as the sole inheritors of righteousness.

Greatness is the willingness to deal with these disturbances and to cope with this unrest, and not merely to put up with it either, shamefaced in cowardly fashion, tolerant with a bitter smile turning the corners of the lips down, but exceedingly glad, with a growing understanding of why more is possible, and finally with the knowledge that only in one garden does the disturbance of More come with the surprise of joyful laughter and the garden gate cannot even accidentally be closed to it, and only in one park does the unrest make itself felt as a mysterious pleasure, so that a greater abundance of life cannot harm our life and the visitor is always welcome.

Or let me hear your point of view. How would you put it?

As soon as mediocrity sees itself as the be-all and the end-all, catastrophe breaks in upon it, thank goodness, to save it from desuetude. But how silly this sounds when we recall that the additional experience was only turned into catastrophe by force of the self-indulgence of those eventually struck, Our laziness one moment causes us aggravation the next moment and there is such a thing as the true path, the clear stream, the happy medium, the time of our life.

Moments or epochs.

As soon as the superior talent judges mediocrity as beneath it in value, the new cutting off the old, the Chosen damning the Called, mission down on vocation, monstrosities are born, atrocities come into being, there is ferocity and desolation. But what can we expect if we cut ourselves off from our roots, from fantasy and folklore, from the established values of the past?

These established values will ruin us, because we made of ourselves rickety, clattering things, and so these ancient rules, this status quo we despise must appear despicable to us,

Judaism: where it clings to itself, refuses the visitor, will not accept any More, Christianity must harm it. Christianity, when it rounds itself out and becomes self-satisfied, rejecting the other one, must be scourged by Islam. Each one comes in the guise of More. Each one wears an unpleasant mask because it visits disrespectfully and because the host extends no welcome.

66

But there is such a thing as world without end, as eternity now, as life that goes on unstoppable.

There is such a one as the truth and the light, the word and the life and the way.

That there is such a one, this is probably the most disturbing fact and the greatest cause of unrest. Not that we believe it, but that it is so. Our believing it moves us into the relevant sphere, so that the disturbance and unrest may profit us and become peace and rest for us, but whether we believe it or not, the fact exists. The disturbance excites and entices us, the unrest leaves us wasted and dissatisfied,

That there has always been such a one, that is a great source of interest. No time in the past can be imagined or recalled when such a one did not exist. Heraclitus, Mencius, Melchisedek knew it, we know it now, that such a one has always existed. And while we keep our gaze turned to the past, do we not wonder, will such a one always exist?

The truth has always existed. The way has always existed. So has the word. And these were one. The light has never gone out and never will go out. The word has always been spoken.

Nevertheless everything has changed. And everything always changes. Whatever is or was or will be is one thing or another and such a thing is man. Such a thing too is the spirit.

The way and the life have always existed in order to be. That was their reason for existing. Reason is such a thing that the life existed through it, because of it.

So the life without reason is as impossible and as un-thinkable and as unimaginable as the life not existing, The life has always existed and has always had reason to exist, and that reason is being.

But nothing can be unless it is one thing or another, since being as such, in itself, makes no sense. Being one thing or another however does make sense, and sense results from a plurality of things.

The word has always existed in order to be one thing or another so that this may make sense. Sense is the achievement of the word. It is also the achievement of the Life and of the way.

But what sense does each of these make?

The light exists in order to be one thing or another which makes sense to our eyes or visible sense. Visible sense means the light of day, or daylight. It means one or the other depending on whether we perceive it, in which case we call it the light of day, or whether we see it, in which case it is daylight. Visible sense means daylight when we see it and the light of day when we perceive it. Seeing is of one thing or another while perception rests in itself. This is why we say that we see and perceive, that we know and understand, since both sustain and enrich us.

The life exists in order to be one thing or another so that this makes sense to our nerves or tangible sense. Tangible sense means the felt emotions or feeling. It means one or the other depending on whether we feel it, in which case we call it the felt emotions, or whether we recognize it, in which case it is feeling. Tangible sense means feeling when we recognize it and the felt emotions when we feel it. Again, recognition is of one thing or another while feeling rests in itself. Both recognition and feeling compare to seeing and perception as knowledge and understanding.

The truth exists in order to be one thing or another which makes sense to our reflexes or imaginable sense. Imaginable sense means the image of reality, or imagination. It means one or the other depending upon whether we think it, in which case we call it the image of reality, of whether we reflect upon it, in which case it is imagination. Imaginable sense means imagination when we reflect upon it and it means the image of reality when we think it. Reflection is upon one thing or another while thought rests in itself. Reflection and thought are as knowledge and understanding.

The way exists in order to be one thing or another which makes sense to our judgment, or reasonable sense. Reasonable sense means the perfect idea or perfection. It means one or the other depending on whether we use it, in which case we call it the perfect idea, or whether we abide by it, in which case it is perfection. Reasonable sense means perfection when we abide by it and it means the perfect idea when we use it. We abide by one thing or another while use rests in itself. Both of these are as knowledge and understanding.

The word exists in order to be one thing or another which makes sense to our belief, or credible sense. Credible sense means the work of love or myth. It means one or the other depending on whether we do it, in which case we call it the work of love, or else we act it out in which case we call it myth. We act one thing or another out but doing, or what we do, rests in itself. Both again are as knowledge and understanding.

*

Myth as the work of love:

On one hand we have myth in the flesh, a contemplative entity, the example, and this has become available to us due to the work of love as we previously illustrated, and on the other hand there is myth as the work of our own love, as we set the example; but in this chapter I intend to understand myth not from one side or the other but simply as the work of love, irrespective of whose love or of the source of it.

Love can be spoken of in terms of power. As such it needs, like any other power, the wherewithal to realize its potential, and this we call matter. Given a certain kind of matter, drawn from one or another sphere of existence or supplied by a type of experience, love realizes itself as works of man, which sounds vague enough and has to be left like that at the moment, but given matter at all, in its basic nature, as the sum total of all particles of resistance, love realizes it – self-powerfully as myth.

Or, instead of power, we may choose in love its principle of selection. That love is applied and then invested in one thing or another, passing from lesser to greater, progressing from lower to higher, this gives it a certain lifespan, a limited productivity with respect to whatever seems made for it or opposed to it, and in such cases the principle of selection needs to be manipulated from without, by a consciousness not involved in it, and usually such a consciousness shares the limited lifespan of the love it involves. If love's principle of selection is to remain intact, so that love at a certain time may be effective, sometime and somewhere, love has to, or must be allowed to, insist on its own free choices. Attraction and repulsion in such cases make no primary difference but they are dealt with when the choice has been made. The principle of selection as choice therefore operates in no binary realm, where a struggle ensues and competition is overcome, but it unfolds itself, or reveals its origin, where a plurality of equivalent entities holds sway. It operates there infallibly. The selection process cannot be reversed and once a choice is made it cannot be unmade. Of course neither would anyone ever want to unmake such a choice, since it fulfils and completes, leaving the person totally changed, not conscious of such a thing as a state previous to, or outside of, the chosen one, as happens in the case of partial selection in a binary realm.

The infallible choices of love are mythic. This means that whether we view them one at a time, several at a time, or all at once, which is to say universally, worldly or cosmically, they put us in touch, or keep us in touch, with our origin and end.

In the third place, after powerful love and choice love, I want to consider disinterested love, or love that works independently of the interest we have or take.

Nothing can interest us unless it can lay claim on our attention and on our energies at once. Our attention must be made to endure. Neither can we take an interest in anything unless it holds out a promise of permanence and of a distinct pleasure.

Once our interest is aroused however, it begins to make a critical difference to how we know ourselves, and in this way it highlights any knowledge we have of ourselves. This is why boredom can be so deadly, because along with a lack of interest comes a lack of self-knowledge, of self-consciousness and self-awareness, leaving only a dull sense of somehow not being other things when for a change it nearly looks as though we might be. An indifferent existence, a scandalous proposition while we love, suddenly seems desirable, and what makes boredom so deadly is that we somehow cannot quite seem to realize entirely this indifferent existence. A niggling remnant of life confronts our attempt at total dissolution, it even outrages us at times, all because we have this absurd notion of a happy death of mind fixed in our body, or of a happy death of body fixed in our mind. If we only knew how lucky we are that this nagging bit of life is still available to us, in case we should choose to love.

Disturbances that arise out of, or document, these foiled attempts at suicide of mind or body, (not of self), such as hysteria, paranoia, certain wasting diseases which are then illustrated by the flesh in terms of illness and sickness, etc, need an investment of love, as an example, before the inflicted individual can rise out of his condition. This love must be disinterested.

Take an invalid, as a philosophical case. Not a man with a broken leg but an individual whose search for validity has centred exclusively on himself and who therefore, by dint of this self-centred 'interest' lacks all validity. His search is bound to become more intense as his failure becomes increasingly apparent to him. His organism or his mentality goes wild. Eventually there must be a breakdown, with death of body or death of mind, always the one opposite to the one that was striven for, and then to the external observer a peace sets in, a solution has been found, a cure effected, when in reality a last spark of vitality, such an insult to the morbid individual, has been snuffed out. The dead mind consists of a finite number of routines, or the dead body is made of mere flesh, with a weight that can increase or decrease, an a-appearance that alters conditionally.

This grim picture of invalid existence illustrates effectively the characteristic foil and spur for a disinterested love, Since the invalid's capacity for interest is totally taken up, by an inverted sense of self, any other interest, brought towards him from without, can only strike him as a further infliction to which he must react. Precisely because he has set himself to negating his individuality, the difference between himself and other individuals – which is not to be confused with his personality, the way he is social, unique, one among many – he cannot bear to have his attentions solicited in favour of any discriminate circumstance, which would always at least accompany or be part of a love that was not specifically disinterested.

Keep in mind that individuality is itself basically a comparative value, and that such a thing as 'one individual' makes little sense, while personality has value from within one person.

And we do want to know about disinterested love not in order to add to our list of analytical data but because we want to learn how to do it. We want to learn how to cope successfully with hysteria and melancholy in our-

73

selves and others. We want to be able to keep ahead of mordant isolationism, morbid revisionism, moribund criticism, in our own nature or as directed towards us, towards anyone or from anyone else's nature.

So first we have to realize that love cannot be initially disinterested. From the start it has to take part. This means that in the cases we illustrated it cannot help but arouse a reaction. Once we have the reaction, to love that is not disinterested, we have what it takes to come up with disinterested love, that is the long and the short of it.

The mechanics of this may be studied.

When our partial love is rejected, not love is rejected but its partiality. We have explained why. It remains for me to acquiesce to this rejection in order to be capable now of disinterested love. If I feel that my love was rejected, which feeling could only be based on misjudgment, I will either hate or stop loving. If I stop loving I espouse individuality. If I hate, I aggravate all the conditions of individuality. So my intelligence has to stand by me, to remind me that my partiality, the partiality of my love, was rejected , not love or my love or even myself.

But what is disinterested love like? Or what is love like insofar as it is disinterested?

In spite of conditions it does not interfere with them. In the face of adverse circumstances, it nevertheless manages to grow. The end to which it applies itself does not lie outside of itself but when I love some thing or someone in a disinterested fashion, I am careful of our common humanity. Humanity is the essence of being, so whatever is, one thing or another, shares with me in a common humanity; consequently love that is disinterested makes no difference and seeks no difference between me and what I love but limits itself carefully to how we are one.

The only additional distinction to be drawn is between disinterested love that returns repeatedly to a partial love, leaving its object of common humanity after a time, perhaps on having completed a task we have set ourselves or on having gained a temporary state of consolation and relief; between this and the disinterested love that goes on to seek and further the special advantage and personal benefit of the one we love. Naturally this can only be the case with human or divine beings, since we cannot, as human beings, entrust ourselves to that which is less than ourselves. But the special advantage we can gain for someone else through disinterested love is a place in our hearts, while the personal benefit we can make available for someone else is a special personal relationship. Consequently what is built up is the fellowship of man, and myth is created.

The fellowship of man, which is myth at its most fundamental, is itself based on disinterested love, and those who wish to partake of this fellowship continue to love one another in disinterested fashion and so as to further each other's livelihood.

But this is my livelihood, that wherever I go I am welcome and whatever I do I am accepted. You cannot dictate to me the nature of my livelihood nor can I direct yours for you. Those whose livelihood is material cannot possibly understand this and we should not try to make it clear to them. For them myth is a lie and money a foundation. Nevertheless we cannot help them come out of themselves and be otherwise since that would be going against their nature. So we let them sleep in their blindness.

*

The worst fate is not to love and then not to know we are loved, because then we have no myth as nourishment and none to protect us.

*

Myth as nourishment:

What are we waiting for while we refuse to love?

Do we want to be loved first, to know that it can be done?

But we are always loved. Love is such a thing that a human being can never be without it.

Or perhaps we want to feel good. We feel terrible and as soon as we feel better we will begin to love. Does that make sense? It does sometimes. Here at least we trust, that eventually we will feel better, and any trust at all makes sense.

Myth nourishes when we love nonetheless.

We do not wait, before we love, until we feel good or until conditions are right as we would judge them to be right, because loving is the most worthwhile thing to do under any circumstances – and then, because we remember that love nevertheless means eventual myth as nourishment.

There is a definite state of being spiritually undernourished. Analysis of it is possible in terms of sense deprivation. This means that a person's sense apparatus itself lacks the wherewithal to function. It does not mean that insufficient sense stimulus is available. We stimulate the senses from without, in order to increase sensation or to make it more manifold. But the sense apparatus itself, in which all our senses are rooted and which may be referred to as the brain stem (distinguishing here too between metaphor and the flesh) needs to be directly manipulated, by will or intellect, if it should happen that here, for one reason or another, no growth goes on or progress is being resisted.

Just as we can speak of impairment to the senses, meaning that our eye is not clear or our ear not sound, so we speak of damage to the brain stem, implying that our sense apparatus, that from which springs our courage and capacity for sensation at all, is to some extent, or perhaps even altogether, not in use. It helps to describe the nature of the thing when we emphasize that in its case a lack of use means damage, in the same way as use means spontaneous use. We move along relatively uncharted ground here. Damage to the brain stem can be discussed. Mechanical sensation, which is sensation not springing from our sense apparatus, can be described. Then, when we speak of sensation normally we imply its mainspring from a common organic origin, but if we compare it to mechanical, or blind sensation, we might stress that sensation is live, or more specifically, normal.

Damage to the brain stem may be due to organic causes, even to a presence of organic causes, where all causes should be natural, and where consequently a sensible transformation would be required, directed from without but generated from within, to set matters right and to make the brain stem well. A marvellous choice of words, really: to make the brain stem well. Because if it is well then it does well, and if it does well, then it wells. Think of the brain stem as the fountainhead of sensation. In a perfect sensation, an inner generation of sense and an outer impression of sense, sense pulse and sense datum, are one and inseparable, though they may be distinguishable, as in the case of a symbol or an instance of metaphor. While on the topic of treatment and cure, or in the case of the brainstem, of healing, it should be mentioned that while an outward direction of sense can be brought to bear in such a way that an inward generation comes about, this success of live sense will cease, the flow of crude sense will cease again, where subsequent sensation is not followed up then spontaneously from within by intellect or will. The brainstem, our sense apparatus, can be healed, but it remains well only in use. Mechanical sensation indulged in up to then must in a certain sense be unlearned and discarded. Live knowledge must take its place. Extinct knowledge, which could only build up and accumulate, monumentally and to gigantic proportions as we see when we look about us today, can not be kept up and must be allowed to disintegrate. It leaves a sensible shell, a natural face-saving device, and live knowledge then installs itself, or is instituted, where this shell, or anagram, holds sway.

No wonder therefore, that live knowledge 'looks no different' from extinct knowledge, while being quite otherwise.

Damage to the brain stem may also be due to neglect, to a lack of appropriate use, to an insistence on mechanical sense, all three amounting to the same, again considering, and helping to explain, what we mean by sense apparatus. One insists on mechanical sense when making a point in any other than a tentative way. Statements of fact based on points of view are already damaging. Laws promulgated on the basis of hypotheses put forward do further damage. Edicts enforced due to primitive belief can finish the job. The ambition to lock mechanical sense into a self-explanatory system or to present it in toto as a self-perpetuating doctrine, has blinded whole generations through the ages. Mechanical sense attracts as a promise of control over everything; it appeals as a final freedom from want and hardship and it evaporates as soon as the energy of him who seeks to attain it is spent. It also excites as an infinite source of criticism. Then it captivates, because we mistake its unity for oneness and so we are led astray, away from our common down-to-earth concerns here in the light of day, where all sense should eventually culminate.

Even the concept of mechanical sense, entertained for one second, detracts from the normal root of sense perception and in order to return, we need to resign ourselves to an order imposed from without. Such an order will always eventually become available to us, but each time as an imposition, and what makes all the difference is whether we quarrel with it and come to grief or give in to it and get nowhere – or, as the third and recommended possibility, we mythify it, in resignation, which means that we confess to an impairment of our senses and to a damaged sense source.

How does this mythification of an imposed order work? The order will be, in opposition, universal, worldly or cosmic and then, upon our settled dedication of our energies to the task, in apposition, the supposed order a.) suits us as a given frame of reference; b.) entertains us as a supplied backdrop, and c., fills us with a ready content. We cannot decide which of the three above mentioned orders is to be imposed upon us, but we can discern which one is being imposed, and so we may act accordingly. The universal order, which suits us as a given frame of reference if we let it, and if we neither try to outsmart the way it depresses or avoid the way it reproaches, may be copied and applied to ourselves inventively. The inventions we come up with serve as products, which means that others may employ them to nourish their senses. We ourselves nourish our senses during the process of production.

The worldly order, which entertains us as a supplied backdrop if we allow it, and if we neither rebel against aspects of it nor become part of any of it, may be imitated and applied to ourselves creatively. The creations which are the outcome or issue of this are then available for others to enrich their senses, Just as our own senses are enriched during the creative process.

The cosmic order, which fills us with a ready content if we permit this, rather than raising formal objections or indulging ourselves mindlessly, may be repeated and applied to ourselves effectively. As a result of this we are conditioned , or in condition, and this has a similar, repeated effect on others, helping them to get into condition, which is a structural principle. Our senses are limited and bound, so that they may thrive, rather than dissipating themselves and leading into temptation.

I would like to emphasize here again that as far as life and love are concerned, since we cannot think or feel in any way 'beyond' them or outside of them, as though a dead or hateful thing could observe and study life or instruct us about love, we must avail ourselves of the truth that a human being always grows and that our humanity all the time progresses, moving towards growth, so that regression excludes humanity and a lack of growth prevents and stops human being, Humanity is the essence of being and human being is humanity in growth. A human being therefore may be helpless and lost but cannot be annihilated; may be weak and in despair but cannot be utterly destroyed. And when we speak of nourishment in this context of myth, we must remember that it involves repair, sustenance and increase, all three, with the implications of fault, burden and path. When we say that myth nourishes when we love nevertheless, we proceed on the understanding that a.) we all make mistakes and that we are willing to take our medicine, whether in mind, body or soul; that b.) burdens exist for a good reason and to some worthwhile end, so shrugging them off or cursing a supposed task master is not necessarily in our best interests, compared to a shared bearing of the burden, making it light; and that c.) it lies in our human nature to reach out and to suffer, to extend and to experiment, to want more and to have it all, and that we do not want to do this like fools but in the wisdom of children.

Myth as nourishment then means all three. I have given actual personal examples, as usual, this time in terms of our common sense apparatus, because disciplined and orderly sensation lies at the very beginning of the myth-making process and is central to its conception as nourishment, but of course other examples are available. What matters is that they are supplied from the fullness of one's life.

*

Good poetry inspires, there's no way out.
A certain frame of reference – sparkling trees,
the rolling lilt of blackbird on a branch
and cunning insects, tasting air like music –

offers some refuge, but no tender light.
For this you risk the terror of the babe.
Bend low to touch your forehead to its cheek
and breathe the scent of pure humanity.

*

Music foreshadowed,
the throb and thrill behind leaded glass,
mellow, the buttery light from streetlamps,
the clatter of vats on cobbles;

a ghost car rushing,
wings of whippoorwill brushing
aside the blue cloud from grey sky
and the longing to be young for a moment.

*

Purple pansies line the plot,
sweet William and forget-me-not.

82

Sit still, reflect; taste of death,
pollen in each wasted breath.

Anger in each clenched fist,
poor psyche by the spirit kissed.
Catch the sun; oh see it melt –
know how gods of Hellas felt.

*

Myth as nourishment – cryptically love nevertheless, or the mythification of an imposed order, an order that can be universal, worldly or cosmic – none of this can feel quite comfortable to our understanding unless we have at our disposal, ready at heart, a certain concept of human being from birth to bliss and a distinct image of human being from birth to death, so that the two of these as one, in love, make it possible for us to deal with such a thing which is actually not a thing at all, but a real human being. One may not be accustomed to differentiating between human being and a human being or human beings, and indeed one may refuse to ever take the trouble or go to that length, but in that case one forfeits the right to a complete reality as a human being oneself. Clear thought and distinct imagination are not possible except in pursuit and ultimate actual achievement of such a complete reality, while birth, bliss and death remain confused notions and arbitrary experiences for us, while our love cannot operate and function towards a oneness of the two.

But how do we gain such a concept and such an image, both fundamental and essential to our understanding of a growing human being in growth, ourselves included? How can I avail myself of the best that there is in order to gain the most and greatest that is possible for me?

In one form or another we have all asked that question. Indeed in the latter of the two formulations above, human beings and people are alike. But people strive to be popular and they aim to survive while human beings want to live as they espouse humanity. This is the great divide. We are either popular or else human and while we are one we cannot be the other. No use suggesting that part of us is popular and part human or that we have streaks of each in us. While we are human we are entirely so, through and through, because that is what it means to be human, and all our capacities are enacted, our proclivities installed. Our popularity would begin not by our realizing a latent potentiality, as though we always 'had it in us' but by our not being human any more. Neither can we be human in comparison to, or in competition with, popularity, because on one hand humanity must set and meet its own standards, which are ever renewed, and on the other hand human beings tolerate people and are kind to them and they have no ambition to change them or make them in any way like themselves.

But this kindness and tolerance is based on human beings and people being in one aspect alike, as we mentioned earlier, which is the desire for increase. Both want to be more and have more, but the difference comes in when we ask: be more and have more what? A quick way to sum it up would be to point out that people want to be what they have or must be what they have, while human beings want to have what they are and they must have what they are, so in a sense people begin with what they have or have not, while human beings begin with what they are or are not. This is easy to understand and not difficult. The human desire for increase stems from what we are born with and

84

relates to what is given to us here and now. We find out what we are in order to invest it in what we can be, and this investment is what we do, in addition to finding out what we are. If we were people, we would find out what was available for us and we would gain as much of this as we could, in order to be one thing or another, because as people we would want to be things, possibly a thing, and we would never be quite happy or satisfied for very long because this would after all not be entirely possible. It is however entirely possible for human beings to achieve their end since they will always be more than they have, considering that human being is eternal and that each human being is finite, so that the continuing human and finite desire for increase is eternally satisfied.

This is impossible to grasp for the popular mind which lacks the relation between the finite and the eternal. It divides the finite into natural and supernatural, physical and metaphysical, and either rejects one of each duality, which can be a life-long occupation in itself, such as taking a stand on nature against supernature, or vice versa; on the metaphysical against the physical, or vice versa; or, instead of rejecting one of each duality, it institutes one in terms of the other, or 'in' the other, and this is where matters become entirely too complicated and involved for our present undertaking.

The relation between the finite and the eternal is mythic.

*

The mythic relation:

In relation to the eternal and to eternal life each human being is finite and lives for a time. But take that relation away and nothing remains of a human being except what we imagine and think of the thing we call human being. So the difference between human being, of which we are all capable and a human being, such as you or I, is a relation to eternal life.

Naturally we would all like to be human beings in addition to being human, but a dry scientific treatise like this is liable to cut us off. As a matter of fact a great deal seems to conspire to cut us off all the time. And what puts us off most, if we want to be perfectly honest about it, is the very next suggestion, from whatever quarters, that: 'You should be a human being.'

The point of the matter is that we cannot and will not be constrained to take up relations with that which stands in reality for liberty and freedom. Not only freedom, but liberty too. Not mere liberty, but freedom too, from which it rises, like the dew from the grass in the morning.

Not a very conventional view of liberty, this, and we put a rather unusual construction on it at the moment, letting freedom precede it rather than making it depend on policies of popular justice, but never mind. We will soon get the hang of it.

Freedom giving birth to liberty in one sense and berth to it in another, that is how we should like to put it.

In this sense liberty is enjoyed by a person as one person, as someone who depends entirely on personality and continually creates that personality, including nothing general but involving everything that is particular.

In that sense, when freedom gives berth to it, liberty affords opportunity and creates choices.

In short we not only want to be free, but we want to act free too, consummate action, because we feel like it and because we seem to have a natural propensity for it. But consummate action gains ends, there is no getting around that, this end or that end, so that where previously we spoke of love nevertheless we now mention surpassing love – to get us into the right way of things.

In order to gain some particular end, through consummate action, we must be at liberty to fail or succeed. No reward or punishment may be incumbent upon, or attached to, the success or failure of the thing, because these remain arbitrary,

Our reason for achieving a particular thing in the first place is primarily surpassing love, the expression and sharing of that love, which comes with the undertaking and not with the success or failure of the undertaking. One is tempted to say that at least secondarily our reason would be the success of the thing in hand, that it falls out the way we planned and according to our rules and aims for it but in reality reason has nothing to do with this and just does not come into it. Whether I actually get this or that done, whether or not I do it well and how much or how little I do, can and should remain quite independent and free of my original reason for taking it up too.

So we may finally formulate consummate action as entailing a liberal deed.

Any doing that is not couched in knowing, that is not part and parcel or a detail of consummate action, attempts to involve some spurious reason or reason on a false pretext, and because it must fail at this, rather fundamentally, we call such doing sacrificial and either should try to avoid it in the first place by setting our sights on surpassing love from the start or we ought to be overwhelmed at first notice by the overriding effects of mercy.

Consummate action entails, by definition, a liberal deed. Without such a deed, action remains commensurate and while it may illustrate or signify love, it does not surpass. We may act at will but no one else will be any the wiser for it. We may act from our intellect but it will do no one else any good. What good commensurate action does the actor can be discussed elsewhere,

Consummate action entails a liberal deed, but by the same token does every liberal deed remain a detail of consummate action. What we do liberally remains limited and conditioned. Of course these limits must be set and these conditions dictated by the one who does what he does, otherwise there can be no personal responsibility. Where anyone else holds us responsible, we must beg to differ and possibly excuse ourselves. Whatever we do according to limits and in line with conditions – enough said; or in agreement with limits and conditions not originally and currently our own, is not done liberally but vicariously, where we follow tradition or custom, official prescription or elemental necessity.

At the risk of making ourselves unpopular we still have to point out that there can be no such thing as a consummate action or as the liberal deed. Liberal doing by definition has to remain particular just as consummate action has to remain general. The entire thing, whether we look at it from the view of someone who is engaged in it through a liberal deed or through the eyes of someone who participates in it as consummate action, is referred to as <u>the mythic relation</u>.

Now whatever difference we make through our doing, whether we fry a trout or rule an empire, is bound to injure someone and lay up a store of guilt for us if our cause is not genuine. We recognize a genuine cause however not by questioning our intentions, which can be structured on the spot to meet the absurdest demands without loss of face, or through interrogation of our moods, which can be mass-produced at the drop of a hat to satisfy the most spurious requirements without the least twinge of conscience, but by the way we supply it and due to the fact that we are supplying it. What we recognize in ourselves as genuine cannot help but be so, and when it comes to a genuine cause we simply supply that through an impulse of spontaneous goodwill. Spontaneous and supply do not contradict or exclude each other, but one follows the other and we can take that for granted. That it fails to comply with the law of mechanics is neither here nor there. Of course if we cannot come up with a genuine cause, then what we have in mind or at heart should be left undone – until such a time, perhaps, as we come up with a genuine cause. Timing is of the essence when it comes to doing. Place is wrapped up with that. Crimes are immature deeds. Premature deeds are sins. Mistakes are untimely deeds.

But the only difference between a success and a failure, when it comes to doing one thing or another from a genuine cause, is whether it meets a particular need or with general approval. The same thing done can fail one moment and succeed the next, may meet a particular need in one century and with general approval four hundred years later. What difference does that make specifically to the one who does it, whether it amounts to a success or a failure? None whatsoever.

The sacrificial deed, by comparison, is done for reward or merit. We do it for public approval or private gain, and we love one thing or another, usually without knowing or admitting it. But such doing falls outside of our present sphere of interest, since it cannot be mythic and we only mention it because commonly it is discussed in similar language even though its cause, or more specifically, our cause in its case, is not genuine but interested. The critical choice therefore is not between doing a thing liberally or sacrificially but rather between our maintaining an individual interest, bent on success or supplying a genuine cause, irrespective of success or failure.

Most familiarly one comes across sacrificial doing in the interest of freedom and of an individual freedom; but liberal doing is not possible unless we are free and unless we have personal freedom. So freedom is attempted through the one and never really gained, while it is a prerequisite for the other; and it is not really the same freedom either,

What should be discussed at greater length is what we called the genuine cause for a liberal deed. How can we supply it? What can we do within ourselves so that what we do out here does us good rather than merely changing the appearances of things?

That aspect of the mythic relation which may be perceived at the start of a liberal deed and to which we refer as the supply of a genuine cause, can be described as an act of witnessing. What we are is put at the service of what we are about to do. We are saying: I am going to do this because of the fact that I am and because of who I am. Now the fact that I am is a thing of joy and of gladness, so this goes into the relation. But far from just lending it an emotional colouring, this joy and gladness can actually be seen to operate as the mainspring of our undertaking, as the key that unlocks the difficulties to let us escape from our dilemmas and as the infallible force of persuasion that makes our path straight.

We bear witness, in addition, to who we are, one or the other person in particular, you or I for instance, by holding ourselves responsible for this gladness and joy rather than disowning it and flying in the face of the deity or provoking those we might love through gleeful insolence.

The joy and gladness that stem voluntarily from our being may exceed all expectation and surmount every obstacle, all misery and sadness, but only while we remain responsible for them and refrain from mechanics and magic.

We have after all undertaken to do something and consequently we have met with a degree of resistance. Things do not naturally want to be done. They prefer to remain unchanged in themselves. Nothing is the matter with them, so why should anything be done with them? As soon as we begin to do, it turns out that something is after all the matter. When we set out to do something with individual persons they often insist that nothing was the matter with them until we came along with our infernal will to do something, and they may well be right, if indeed we treated them mechanically or magically, or if we were critical of them, or if we abused them in order to disabuse ourselves, or a thousand such instances of mischief, with this one element missing, namely our responsibility for what we feel. Let us call it a conscious awareness of the fact that it is we who feel it, by choice, and that no one else makes us feel it or has done anything to make us feel it. Neither should the resistance that is offered by things, their material reluctance to be changed, be transferred by ourselves to us, as more material resistance, then perhaps to be sacrificed to our will – but due to our being voluntarily and responsibly joyful and glad in the face of this resistance, we make it possible for the humanity that is the essence of all being, our own being included, to show itself and become one, as human being. When we deal in this way not only with things but with individual persons, what shows itself and becomes is one or more human beings.

And of course in our dealings with individual persons becoming human beings, two or three together, we may supply the greatest and most wonderful cause, which has ever remained impossible for the great ones of the earth and of the world, because they limited themselves to human being and to its evolutionary supremacy over humanity in all things, gaining a foothold and conquering territory by way of mechanics and magic, of the psyche, the sense and the sun, and we have dealt with these scientifically as systems, the psychosomatic system, the logical system and the solar system, in separate books.

But from humanity to human being is a step, a cultural step and one that leads to civilization, for a time, then back to the beginning, and one might well be excused for espousing a belief in the everlasting recurrence of the same things as the highest order of human achievement in understanding if it had not become possible for human beings to exist and live.

This particular and crucial change, from human being as personified and characterized by you or me, to human beings, you and me, is the one we record presently in terms of this mythic relation, liberality based on freedom, cause supplied to deed, surpassing love and exceeding gladness.

And do not say that the freedom on which this liberality is based was gained by a cultivating effort and a civilizing strain, because these have always been seen and experienced as ends in themselves, vicarious and representative, official and professional; famous, prestigious and somehow predestined. But this freedom was gained in spite of them. Therefore, and only therefore, do these efforts and strains have something to be said for them, namely for the type of resistance they made available so that one might work out one's own humanity and be free.

What we are is put at the service of what we are about to do. The material resistance of the thing we do, its reluctance to change, is not again resisted, but becomes fuel for our joy and momentum for our exceeding gladness. It does us no good to pretend that we like this resistance, the natural revolt of the closed being, nor should we try to make a virtue out of tolerating or ignoring it. What matters is that we recognize it and use it up. If a man says to you: Speak no more! you may well decide to keep quiet, but probably you are not finished with him yet. He may look for rest within you.

We supply the cause from within our being and from within our human being. If our being is not human, but animal for instance, this will make no sense to us, because only human being responds to an appeal within or without. From within our human being, where all we possess is stored, a cause becomes available, but not independent from what we intend to do. I may intend to build a house. Such an undertaking will undoubtedly tax many of my faculties, but there is no need for it to tax me. If it does, and to the extent that it does, I have no cause and my activity will be irrelevant. The mythic relation will not fully operate.

A cause becomes available but not independently from what we want to do because of the humanity we share in common with what we want to do. The nature of this cause, remembering that we aim at a result in time, is mystical.

I may wish to help my wife with the washing-up or I may intend to shift the burden of belief in 'this generation'; the need for a genuine cause will be equally apparent if I want to help and not hinder, so as I apply myself to the task in hand, I watch for the response of my nature and for any reaction within my nature or being. That there should be a response sooner or later is hardly surprising since it lies in my nature, in my human being, to express itself and to unite itself with other samples of human being, to associate with other natures, as we pointed out in a previous chapter. As for reactions within my nature, these may be ascribed to the usual trial and error method of experimental advance in time. My reason for watching for the response of my nature and for a reaction within my nature is that I wish to supply a genuine cause to the task in hand, to the end I mean to achieve; not so that my efforts will succeed but so that the task, once accomplished, will have done some good and no damage, which is to say that it will have made me and whoever else is involved more of a human being rather than merely changing appearances for us or altering our lifestyles.

A response of my nature might be a mood of elation or a moment of terror. I would not let these pass but I would assume they were meant for me in particular rather than being connected generally with the nature of my task, with the washing-up or the creation of philosophy. The difference between the menial task and the great work does not concern us here, they would both be equally in need of a genuine and sufficient cause if they were to contribute in a singular fashion to me and to you as human beings in growth, eternally related.

A reaction within my nature might amount to an unwillingness to continue because of boredom or a lack of confidence due to a suspected failure; reactions always carry their own inverted causes on their backs, which is why it happens so readily that we fall in with them, and having fallen in, we make so much less of an effort to climb back out than to perpetuate our confinement by self-justification and lame excuse. If I watch, however, and have remained on my guard, I can mechanically steer these reactions in the direction of the task in hand. First however I will have to presume that the boredom and the lack of confidence have nothing to do with the definition of me or of my nature, of my human being, but that they were instigated on the occasion of what I set out to do and that they may on one hand be comprehended as signs of the aptness of my undertaking and on the other hand be perceived as symbols of the appropriateness of my task, of the suitability, to myself, of my attainment. Given this particular presumption, which usually goes against the grain of our individual selves, I may then go ahead and continue with my work, with what I am doing, as well as I am able, without fear of fanciful supererogation or disingenuous self-sacrifice.

In the hope that this will not take us too far afield, we will just mention that this realm of reaction within our nature, of reluctance to change, which is really only of secondary importance in comparison to our responses to which we intend to return shortly; that this very limited and confined state of our being as seen from within lends itself profitably to study as a machine, and that here we may enter the true world of mechanics, of morality and of merit; of duties and rights and techniques: it goes this far and no further. Remember that as an end in itself this world becomes scandalous and unworthy. The responsible actions of a human being among human beings are not even approached by it then. Reactionary activity, when the reactions within our nature to change are taken for values and sanctions and standards, far from allowing a human being to come to fruition, drags even human nature back from its commitment to the individual person and sells out society, for the price of a superficial and loathsome peace-and-quiet, to eventual chaos and catastrophe. The science of mechanics enter into its own however, where our related interests remain strictly limited to our pursuit of the liberal deed within consummate action, where the force of every reaction is guided and geared not towards contemporary success in one field or another but towards the end and goal of our human nature itself, this being a human being and human beings, me and you. In that case we cannot help but do our best and work as well as we can. Merit must retain its relativity to some individual person and cannot be standardized. Morality remains an issue within the context of groups of individuals and people.

Mechanics as a study will curtail its interests to within the sphere of force and counterforce, not to explain any reality in such terms but to reestablish, wherever possible, an equilibrium and an order, again not as an end in itself but as a smoothing of the way. Various techniques by which mechanical problems are solved, from fundamental to diverse, may be communally agreed upon but must be originally applied and there can be no consensus on such application. You will always want to figure out your own way of doing it, whether you seek the kingdom of heaven within you or decide to build a bridge across the stream behind your house. So techniques and disciplines always have to be reinvented or else they become rigours and routines. Rights have to be continually reinterpreted and duties redefined, but never for anyone else, only you for yourself and I for myself, otherwise duties become interferences and rights trespasses. Elevating it to the level of a Nation or a State only aggravates the problem and makes it worse. Once I begin to define your rights for you, you will wish to rebel. Any one who prescribes my duties for me will have trouble on his hands.

Mechanics, morality and merit then have to do with the avoidance of reactionary activity and with the preparation for responsible action, but they do not themselves in any way figure in such action, and neither do their concrete manifestations, which we have summed up under the headings of techniques, rights and duties.

What does figure in such action however, and most critically so, is any response of my nature. We have already put our finger on two possible responses, a mood of elation and a moment of terror, and we have intimated that the nature of the cause we mean to supply is mystical.

Mystical, in this context, implies an alliance and an alignment of all our faculties towards a nervous goal; in other words we practice critique not of one thing or another but of the state of our human being itself , and of its current state, as we find it at the moment. We practice this critique so as to make ourselves, not someone else, conform – for the time being, for the duration of time that it takes to exercise our faculties towards a result (a spontaneous result) – to the matter in hand presently, whatever that may be: a speech to the House of Commons or an act of sexual love. We exercise our faculties towards a result which occurs spontaneously. We have no control over it. We never know <u>when</u> it will be but only <u>that</u> it will be and then that it is.

This spontaneous result is our cause. As soon as we have it we build on it, and we have no decisions to make as to how we will build on it because we are, after all, already committed in that respect, because of what we have in mind to do: our consummate action and our liberal deed, whatever it may be in particular, an attendance at the local garden fête or a period of convalescence after a physical injury.

The response of our nature fuels the critique; and remember that we watched for it. We could not have gone on prior to the advent of such a response.

The response of our nature, by the way, is epiphenomenal in character and secondary, or of a secondary order, leading on to the spontaneous result to our critical exercise, which is phenomenal and primary: phenomenal   in person and of a primary species.

The state of our human being as we find it at the moment – here lies the crux of the matter. We obviously mean to take ourselves as we are in commitment, not in neutral, and the dynamics of our action, the generative drive, precisely because we refused to espouse such a thing blindly, may be placed now, when the time is choice, by ourselves where we deem it singularly appropriate.

We may choose to be as we wish.

We may choose to be happy, lucky or holy. All that matters is that we understand what it is we wish to be. We may not even be in the possession of the right words for it, as long as we understand it. We may choose to be cheerful or glad. What we are then concerns all of us, not just one of us, that is the nature of the happiness or cheerfulness that is imparted to us: not holiness in a cave or luck in a private corner, gladness gleeful in an opinion of my mind. Consequently my happiness will create happiness elsewhere, or subsequently it will do so, but again no connection other than this happiness will be obtainable, and no one will come to me and say: 'Thank you for making me happy', because true happiness is communal,

as is real holiness and thorough blessedness. We cannot
114

have it merely for ourselves, it will not fit, no justice suffices for it that way – but I may have it for all of us and the joy I may ask for with a certainty of receiving it appertains from the start to a multiplicity of concepts and to a plurality of images, so that our very concept of life from birth to bliss is touched by it and our image of life from birth to death is overwhelmed by it.

Of course the luck and the certainty I receive, the joy and clarity, are not states again, and I do not find my state of being changed or transposed to a state of joy and clarity, but they are substantial, and to that extent I too am substantial, so that I could not exclude you even if I tried.

Nor can I say that substantial joy and substantial luck and blessedness are all one thing or another, all emotions, feelings, not even all substances.

They are all mythically discrete.

If it were not so, we would be able to abuse them, and we would abuse them. These what? These – you know, joy and happiness and freedom, all of them substantial.

We consult our present state, of human being, in the name of mythic substance, of which we remain aware, that is the downward look, merciful and compassionate, and then we apply this name, to one or another: happiness, substantial happiness, mythically discreet; or pleasure, substantial, not petty pleasure, and I am happy or pleased as a human being. That is the upward look.

As a human being I cannot exist in the singular – nor in the plural of course, because that would draw defeat down on me and on us, but I am along with you and others.

For human being to be changed into a human being, this change has to be willed, more precisely wished or desired by us, and it must be understood in the name of myth.

*

The name of myth:

We noticed how pleasure, for example, rather than stemming from a self-abuse of the senses or residing in things to be indulged, may be attained insofar as we wish to be pleased or desire to be pleased, not through means but directly; not in time but immediately; for insofar as we wish to be pleased like this we link our substance as human beings to the substance of humanity, which far from ruling us and incorporating us into a state, confirms our particularity, making me more myself and you more yourself, so that we may be more ourselves and our community may grow, not in numbers but in name.

It may in fact be quite clearly observed here how community, as the incorporation of the communal (not this or that community as an incorporation of some communal idea for instance) allows for an application of both name and number (not names and numbers) in such a way as to inculcate the nameless, the not-yet-named, and the countless, or not yet numbered or counted.

What we mean by the name of myth therefore holds itself distinct from label, which is name that has been numbered, and insists on a continuity into that which has not yet been named and on an openness to that which cannot be numbered or counted.

There is more to name than what we call a thing. By the same token, when we know the name of something we can do more than just call it, or refer to it.

If we hope ever to agree on the importance of this, and on the fact that this is so, we ought to gain insight into why one might choose to name something or someone in the first place rather than limiting ourselves to points of reference, as in a system, or insisting on categories, where the least common denominator is eventually sieved out for the sake of a familiar indication.

Because a name is supposed to do both, explain and distinguish.

Mind you, once we have decided that we wish to be part of a system, or of the system, and once our faculties have become geared in that respect, we will have to come up with quite extraordinary definitions to tell one another about what would otherwise have appealed as part of everyday knowledge. And once our understanding is cut down and shut down to the deplorable level of category and rule we will call it mysterious and strange when someone breaks through one of the cells of this prison and catches a glimpse of what would otherwise be the living-room of our home.

Such is the use of the term mystical, when we wish to draw attention to the fact that there is more to a house than the price we would have to pay for it. Indeed there is more, such as the rooms, the roof and the foundation. But then there is also the price; unless of course we were given the house. In such a case price does not enter.

We mentioned in the previous chapter that the cause we supply to consummate action is naturally mystical, which implied a practical critique. We had to make ourselves ready for the spontaneous result, which then turned out, in practice, to be our ability to be what we wish to be, given a substantial understanding.

Now we would call that mystical which we leave behind and aside when we give a new name or do something in a name. Our reason for calling it anything at all is so that we can put it behind us and aside rather than being confused by it as we pursue our aim, and our reason for calling it specifically mystical is that we have to do with customary nerve-satisfaction and habitual nerve-energy, which must be recognized and acknowledged as such if we are to avoid an obfuscation by it of our senses, especially of our feeling, which deals with nerve energy on purpose and is usually held responsible by us for our nerve-satisfaction.

Remember that what we put aside and back as mystical is eventually to be part of, to be covered by, the name we intend to give, and for that reason we do not neglect it or ignore it or destroy it. We only put it on ice. It amounts in totality to everything to which we might so far give a name, but we refrain from giving it a name for the time being because that would harbour it and hold it, while we in fact want to let it be.

However the prime reason for giving a name is an acquisition of knowledge, so presently we are looking for more knowledge. Our body of knowledge wants to grow.

Our senses not only want to sense but they want to increase. We want to add on to them.

And the reason for doing in the name of something, even as we store temporarily the mystical in the name of what is new, is so that any knowledge we acquire becomes part of us and so that our body of knowledge is made flesh.

We may describe the whole process therefore as acquisition of knowledge in terms of the mystical, of the nameless or anonymous by choice and for a purpose, and incarnation of knowledge in the name of the new, or in the new name, which is that to which we now give the new name, calling it Jesus.

Just as in the previous chapter we spoke of a spontaneous result to our practical critique, phenomenal in person, so we may now speak of a voluntary return to our mystical body, noumenal in Jesus.

Our mystical body is our usual body of knowledge but temporarily anonymous. The choice of anonymity must of course be our own and not merely imposed by circumstances as resignation.

It is not we who return to our mystical body. That would be absurd. There is a voluntary return however, and we know it to be voluntary because we have no jurisdiction over it. We are powerless with respect to the time of this return, and of course if we did not trust that there would be a return we could not estrange ourselves from the strange, in fact we would not allow for a strangeness, would not understand the estrangement as ultimately profitable and finally beneficial.

And most of all, I suppose, we would not be able to recognize this return when it occurs. But how silly! Then there would be no return.

But what do we mean, exactly, when we say that our body of knowledge becomes flesh? Do we mean the fruition of Euclidean geometry and Newtonian physics in terms of tractors and nuclear warheads? Not at all. This pertains to the realm of the extinct. It begins in the flesh and ends in it, and it shortens the time. Or do we mean the application of Pauline theological doctrine and of Aristotelian Thomism to the conduct and behaviour of individuals and groups? Not at all. Again these would be allegorical exercises in extinction, and they have value as such, in the sphere of mechanics, merit and morality, of direction, duty and death, in which these three deal and specialize. Now when we live in reality we do not let the world sidetrack us, either by criticizing it or by falling in love with it. And similarly when we know the name of Jesus we do not come into conflict, surely, with Christianity or with any other religion of the world. Such conflict would only lead us wide of the mark and confuse us in our knowledge.

What we do mean when we say that our body of knowledge become flesh is mythically available to us as what we do in the name of Jesus as the existence of reality, or as the existence, if we want to avoid a pleonasm. For Jesus today is the existence, and the existence of whatever is real. And we distinguish between existence and the existence as we do between that which is extinct and that which is live. So in extinction, existence precedes essence, as analogs of the flesh, and when we have to do with the flesh we always deal with it in a guise, basically as one of these two analogs, in existence or in essence; but in reality there is no such thing as *the* flesh, but the existence and the essence are flesh and they are one flesh, in each particular human being, in you and in me.

The separation of the flesh into existence and essence is not real, then, but illusory, and any analogous system is illusory, is a veil, and we can learn to make use of this veil – or rather we can learn to be grateful for it rather than wishing to penetrate or tear it in order to unveil or reveal what we mistakenly presume lies behind it. Nothing in fact lies behind it. There is no such place as behind this veil. Just as there is no such reality as the flesh. But we call it the flesh in order to remind ourselves of what we have left behind.

Or again, the flesh as essence or existence, in one of these two guises, or as something that exists for which an essence is subsequently fabricated in either case, whether structure or profile of extinction, or then as a game is played, where we smartly keep out of the way while the rules unfold themselves, seemingly edifying, slightly entertaining; here in the light of day we will have none of it, call it Science, Art or Sport, depending on whether existence fascinates or essence distracts, or one joins the other; we will have none of it because we know it for what it is; delusion for those who maintain it, illusion for those who notice it as a veil and respect it as such. We will not see through it because for us there is nothing on the other side of it. This veil is itself the limit.

Or you might call it the mirror.

The surface that is always kept polished for our sake so that we know where to stop.

Formal education is Art, Science and Sport. This has been set down before us in our youth, only so that we may be tested. And what if all but one out of a thousand take the veil? What if they look into the mirror and discover another world? If the veil is drawn aside for them and they discover one thousand new veils, and so on, until the darkness takes them, until death parts them? If mirror upon mirror, facet upon facet, charms and enthralls, promising the all it cannot keep, holding out rest that can only be absence of death?

We are not to quarrel with that.

We are not to rack our brains for a world-wide solution, to break our hearts because 'they all go into the dark'. Instead, if we turn away from the flesh, we may first feel lost for the lack of familiar ground, but then we take ourselves off, like a swimmer to the middle of the stream, where we do not construct but we let things take shape; we do not form content but we are form and content in one and act ourselves out; we do not carry a burden and are not carried as a burden but our substance becomes mingled and matched with the substance of everything.

If we want to do anything, we do it for the sake of him who would have us do it and he alone knows, so there we have knowledge. Whatever we do in his name is entirely done and well done, and there is no room for checking the entity and controlling the quality. The fact that we do what we do in his name ascertains the genuine value of our deed. And indeed there is a product. Not this or that;

but there is a product. It has to be described in the language of today, so no use carping, such as: We know all about it, someone else called it this and another one called it that. And the product is not a tractor or a guided missile, is not a formula or a theory, a record time or the prize for a contest, a novel, a symphony or a painting. It must be laid out like this, there is no getting around it, because concepts stifle it and categories choke the life out of it.

The product is what we call flesh, or one flesh, and this is the end product. A human being is god become flesh, to some degree or to some extent. So each human being is eternal. Please note that we do not mention *the* human being, a theoretical construct or an ideal – biological, moral or theological.

This product is what makes one human being discernible to another. Sometimes we wonder how it is that we recognize each other. We have no previous experience for a standard of comparison and certainly it cannot be tested out. And once we have it we can find no trace of its origin but it is itself, wholly and completely.

We come to the conclusion therefore that what we do in the name of him who returns us to our mystical body stands us in good stead as soon as we seek communion.

Communion we define as the coming together of human beings to celebrate their existence in the flesh and to take joy in the fact that they really live. Where speech is involved, this is called communication.

But this celebration, such a communion, is always entirely spontaneous and voluntary. It cannot be planned ahead of time, as an event or a meeting, and needless to say, there is no room for officiation, for behaviour according to rules or for regulated conduct.

Instead there is free association for the sake of an operation of love.

This free association, as it happens, is profitably called the essence of communion and the operation of love is called its existence. We distinguish between the two only for the sake of a continued communion. Neither precedes the other and neither could be studied independently or separate from the other. They are one flesh.

Our awareness as live human beings is at its greatest during communion and so we would naturally wish to propagate it and to establish it as an ongoing thing. This can be done most successfully during our awareness specifically of the essence and the existence of communion while communion goes on.

Free association can be furthered and cherished. It is furthered by reopening any avenues of communication that happen to be closed and by overcoming any barriers to the growth of that association as they turn up and present themselves. Keeping in mind what we are talking about here and what sort of thing we mean, it should not come as a surprise when we hear that the means for reopening avenues of communication reside in the fullest possible acceptance of their closure as a mythic fact and they are not obtained or derived from any remaining openness of communication, rationally or reasonably or logically, nor from anywhere outside the most thorough possible experience of that closure, temperamentally, passionately or mechanically.

The forthright admission, not sadly or as an accusation, of broken-down relations, reopens: not negotiations or dealings towards an eventual and hoped-for free association but free association itself. This is also what is meant by the closure or the breakdown as a mythic fact. There is no getting around it, behind it or past it. Any attempt to do so results in false evidence and in evidence that misleads, so that we usually make the mistake of laying blame that is due to our own initial error at the feet of someone else who cannot have a clue as to what we mean by it, since the evidence by which we go sprang fallaciously out of our own wrongdoing. This wrongdoing stems from our dealing with mythic fact as though it were mere myth or abstract fact. The closure or breakdown, as mythic fact, must be grasped intuitively as a thing in itself that would lend itself to mythic interpretation.

*

Mythic interpretation:

Mythic interpretation is the name we give to the kind of interpretation that deals in itself with a thing in itself which is understood, or perceived, as an absolute opportunity for growth, or as an opportunity for absolute growth, which is the same in this case.

At the moment, for example, although we have discussed free association insofar as it is furthered, our understanding is closed with respect to how it is cherished, and no amount of force of trickery will be able to duplicate what we mean by mythic interpretation, where we freely admit that part of our freedom is gone, in the knowledge that the handicap, as we would call it, is in fact a potential insight or some improvement of intelligence and increase in understanding. Witness for example how Plato discusses the handicap of Socrates in the Apology, where the old man mentions at his trial how in the past a divine daemon has often checked him, held him back even in midsentence, in order, as Socrates believes, to prevent him from acting foolishly, and that now, during the time leading up to his trial and during it, even though he knows his accusers to be malicious and their charges to be false, he has not been held back once. We are shown by Plato how this man Socrates was capable of 'mythic interpretation', and how far from just making the best of a bad thing, as a man of vocation would have done such as those for whom his three accusers allegedly spoke, he actually chooses, and has made a habit of choosing, the obstacle itself as a hindrance favourable to himself and not to be overcome. Actually it would be going too far to say that Socrates interpreted mythically in the same sense as we mean here unless he had at least a presentiment of that one deity which presumably gave evidence of itself at Delphi and also made it possible for him to be beneficially checked and masterfully limited in his behaviour and conduct. I suppose it would be safe to assume that Socrates had such a presentiment, if we go by how Plato presents him, and indeed why should he not. The mythic fact can be more closely approached when we see it in the light of both what Socrates actually did and factually was and what Plato, and other sources, make him out to have done and been, a topic we touched upon in our first chapter on myth as fact. It is after all entirely up to us whether or not we choose to believe that Socrates ever existed in the flesh. Besides, we do not feel that we have to defend anyone's reputation against that of

Socrates; we can let myth and fact speak for themselves. And Plato seems to have defended the reputation of his friend Socrates quite successfully, such as against the popular point of view of Crito, and in the book of that name Socrates instructs his visitor on the inability of ordinary people to do a human being any real harm. They have no unlimited power to do good and consequently no unlimited power to do evil, and hence they act at random.

So now, by use of a kind of science within a science, we have mythically interpreted the block that prevented us from going on directly to a description of how free association can be furthered, first of all by a forthright admission of the curtailment of that freedom and then by an act of mythic interpretation, when the handicap that was, now acknowledged, is replaced by an addition or an amplitude of life.

Free association is cherished, as compared to being furthered, when the mythic interpretation we have both described and demonstrated goes on as a willful activity of love when we love one another.

For in the face of an obstacle we furthered our free association intellectually insofar as the intellect, or rather our intellect, in juxtaposition to our will, preponders, allowing our will to unfold and fuel it; but now, with no hindrance in sight for the time being, our will predominates over our intellect, expecting our intellect to maintain and support it during an activity of special love.

Considering the oneness in flesh of our intellect and will, they are certainly not the same and both are distinct, but one predominates or the other preponders, it makes little difference which, for our present purpose, and also, reconsidering this oneness, the expectations of the one that predominates are never disappointed and the allowances of the one that preponders are never abused.

This should not be compared to that extinct state of affairs when an intellect, or the intellect, went on the rampage until by force of circumstances it found itself circumscribed; when a will, or the will, could not even exist except in opposition and contradiction, and then it either triumphed monstrously or submitted pitifully, while the intellect became blind in its own brilliance.

It should not be compared because the common denominator is missing. The will in extinction and in the flesh was nothing like our will here and now, when we have what it takes to limit our activity to the extent of our own human being for the sake of other human beings and when the enlightenment of our intellect circumscribes entirely and sufficiently; when it ascertains perfectly and completely.

For a change it can happen that will and intellect are indistinguishable, during works of love, when I have your best interests at heart and my own are not neglected. But love works in such a way that our will and intellect are one flesh. It stands to reason that they could not be one until they were one flesh, so this is the reality on which we concentrate. Not in love, but during works of love, are our will and intellect one flesh. There must be a passage of direction or a line of attraction, either one, and the absence of these fills us with trepidation, out of which passage or direction may lead and from which a line of attraction may proceed. In 'fear and trembling' we await the influence or help of some lesser god where one god is

113

ours. Fear attracts and trembling directs. Knowledge of this proceeds from our one god and the understanding of it leads to him.

But our works of love thrive best in the flesh, out here where we live in the eyes of everyone, people and human beings alike. In this sense we can say, in the hope of remaining articulate, that in our works of love our will and our intellect are one flesh in the flesh. But the flesh is of no use, so whatever is in the flesh must be one flesh if it is not to be injured or harmed. Now if we are harmed, we have nothing to worry about because the harm is peripheral and its purpose is a glorious demonstration. Equally if we are injured we are not overly concerned because the injury is superficial and the reason for it is such a thing as a mythic program or plan.

*

A mythic program or plan:

> Death is neither here nor there.
> Socrates knew as much .
> He sat in prison chewing his cud,
> life's pleasures and life's pains forgetting,
> nothing regretting.
>
> When lyrics came to him he dreamt them.
> He looked forward to the big sleep.
> Since then so much has happened.
> Socrates stirs and wakes,
> the earth quakes.
>
> My body sees and hears, is sight
> and hearing, and the rest too,

so that all these become one
in the natural investigation of life.

Let no man torture himself,
or others for that matter, seeking knowledge
through sense, since sense is knowledge,
or by the way of sensation,

for sensation too is knowledge.
My eyes are that part of me
which is called visual knowledge
and my ears are prayer.

To maintain ourselves here, very little is required and
we call it a mythic program or plan. This gives some indication to others of what we are about and lets us proceed and go about our business in relative peace and quiet.

If we use the terminology acquired in the last chapter,
we may say that due to an injury we avail ourselves of a
mythic program so that we may be one flesh in the flesh.
From the popular point of view this looks like terminal
existence and can be countenanced without too much of a
problem. We have to appreciate that people regard all
things, including spirit, from the point of view of the
flesh and it does no good to pretend otherwise. Now the
sort of injury we are talking about here is incurred when
we assume that we know better what is good for people
than they do. But people, to whom we refer as that generation, in line with our science, cannot possibly accept a
live interpretation of anything, and to the extent of my
own popular persuasion my own senses too are extinct,
and far from benefiting from a real challenge, I can only
react and fall back on the person I really am, withdrawing
from extinction, including the infection of it in my

senses. To all intents and purposes I am then, in those senses, blind. Given another unsuitable opportunity, which we might also call a fitting temptation, those blind senses will again make popular judgments, indulging themselves, and me, in prejudice and involving us in bigotry of one sort or another, so that a bare confrontation with reality will have gained me nothing in this respect. The same of course goes for people in general, who can only be held responsible for themselves for a time before they revert to type in order to insist on the popular law of extinction.

The name we give to that which causes the injury, which is either an attempt to propagate extinction by setting up a plausible alternative to reality, or, which amounts to the same, a desire to destroy the various products of extinction in order to make room or time for reality, is criticism, and should be avoided at all cost.The best way to avoid it is to treat extinct things and people with respect, and by making ourselves, with respect to our own extinction, undergo a rigorous and radical critique.

The salient point to be remembered in all cases is that extinction and its products, or its redoubts as I suppose one should say, cannot be opposed, since it is in itself the opposite, and where we come across it, in politics or in poetry, in people around us or in ourselves, we would do well to regard it as a turning-point for us, not as something to be challenged or insulted, removed or broken through .

Nevertheless, where criticism does take place, and where a grain of sand slips into the flesh of the oyster, there we may avail ourselves of a most singular option, which is the creation and manufacture of a mythic program or plan.

Criticism is the inexpediency par excellence. Even a description of it would probably involve us in criticism. That which most successfully furthers our progress on the other hand, and helps us grow, eternally, is a kindly love.

Our response to this preternatural injury therefore, to this injury which we have always both caused and sustained, due to a lack of watchfulness or on account of a soulless action, is by way of this kindly love, and this is the only way of healing the injury, with the added bonus that the fruits of this love may help to sustain more of us, even as in the growing of them we grow ourselves. For us there is therefore both restitution and institution, dispatch and enterprise, both healing and revealing.

And if it should be necessary to say so, we cannot act preternaturally, and there is no way we can set out intentionally to market the fruits of this love by first indulging in criticism for the sake of … but the suggestion is too absurd.

Now that we have filled in some of the background for this mythic program or plan, and have supplied the principle, which is a kindly love in the face of criticism, we may go on and map out such a program or plan, for the sake of those who have never had the good fortune to be involved in one, and we can give various examples and instances where such a thing has been approached and executed in the past.

Take for example the parables of Jesus. Here have actual instances of a critique that stays well ahead of criticism. Insofar as these parables are meant to convey information about the kingdom of heaven, they are mythically programmed and to the extent that they take into account the particular capacities of listeners they are mythically planned. The kingdom of heaven would have made such a difference to the human beings of that day that they would have quite lost themselves and each other in criticism, in faulty being and reactionary becoming, and so these parables manufactured, as it were, a locus vivendi for each and every one who chose to listen and take them in. On account of these then, and within their relative protection and security, the individual person could countenance the approach of the kingdom with faculties alert and a minimum of fear and trembling. There was more to these parables than mythic programming and planning since Jesus delivered them verbally to those whose hearts he knew, which also explains why there was no need to wait for criticism and its cumulative effects, but it is precisely because there was more to these parables than what specifically interests us at the moment that we can accept them as models for what we do have in mind.

First of all we cannot help but notice that we have a prototype here of the kindly love we mentioned earlier, extended by those who are in the know to those who are not in the know; and a separation is shown between those 'to whom it is given to know the mystery of the kingdom of god' and those who are 'outside' (Mk. 4:12). Those who are outside, theoretically first of all, are not dismissed or arrogantly spurned, but on the other hand they are not hypocritically appeased or fanatically provoked either. Their state as sinful and their condition as morally blind is realistically perceived and admitted, and then catered to, in terms of parable and of figures of speech.

Already some four-hundred years earlier, Socrates, in Plato's Crito and Phaedo, distinguishes between the devotees to the philosophical life on one side and ordinary people, who are afraid of death and act at random, on the other side, including temperate people and decent citizens whose virtues are founded on fear and dread rather than on wisdom. And here, too, Socrates is shown to practice no rejection of these ordinary people, and no mollification, but he knows them for what they are, gives them the benefit of his kindly disposition and in the end, either by letting the laws of Athens speak in his favour as at the end of Crito or by offering them an imaginative description of his vision of the real earth as near the end of Phaedo, he creates a kind of mythic program or plan, to inspire himself and those near him with confidence, especially with respect to his soul's immortality and, more from Plato's point of view, to safeguard the mysteries by turning them figuratively out towards ordinary people, in one way or another. Crito in particular, like Thomas four-hundred years later, remains critical to the end and rather curiously finds it just as difficult to decide between the immortal soul and the eventual corpse of Socrates as Thomas cannot readily find it in himself to believe the immortal body of Jesus but he has to touch, to sense, before he accepts reality. But this would get us too far into the realm of wonder and divination.

A theoretical distinction exists therefore between those who know and those who do not know, and the attitude of the former towards the latter must by definition be one of a kindly love, rather than mutual contempt, as Plato's Socrates identifies the trend, or as fire brought down on the heads of the latter, as Peter suggests before he is re-oriented by Jesus. The fact that it 'is given' to some to know the mystery of the kingdom of god, really would seem to imply two things; first of all that one cannot me-chanically supply anyone with the knowledge and then that one can in fact make a difference to those who are not in the know by offering them a figurative representa-tion of the essential knowledge, so that their ignorance might become ponderable and their blindness transparent to them. If this were to happen, they would not, by virtue of such an effect, begin to know and to see, but their igno-rance and blindness would become available to them as something they can deal with and occupy themselves with, in short, so that they can come to recognize themselves as ignorant and blind. And of course those who are in the know would be the first to admit their ignorance on occa-sion and their blindness at times, because they know that this is the only way to turn and begin to know and see.

Eventually we cannot help but rely on this spirit of kindly love to bail us out, when we have sunk as low as we dare or risen as high or gone as far, not in a moral sense of course. It then shows us, this spirit, how to pre-sent ourselves figuratively, which is to say face to face. We learn how to produce semblances of ourselves, how to assimilate the friction that comes with misunderstand-ing, and finally how to account for ourselves in some concrete manner so that our rest is perfected.

That our rest must be perfected from without goes without saying. We can work towards this. We can fully extend ourselves towards a material universe without entering that universe, but we must wait until the time is ripe before our perfection can not only be, but also come to our notice. When it does come to our notice, from without, we have what it takes, remarkably, to render our perfection exquisitely secure .

Exquisite data come to our notice in time. Together we refer to them as exquisite experience. No metaphor is available for this in particular and no parable is possible to signify it because we have to do here not with humanity or human being, nor strictly speaking with any particular human being such as you or I, but with the essential spirit of human life here and now. Where human life ends, more human life begins, that would be a way of putting it, except that it leaves out of consideration the merciful reality of the eternal.

There is no such thing as the sum-total of all exquisite data but they occur at random and we take them for granted. One may also accept them as given, as long as one remembers that the giver gives himself in them.

They are also extremely personal. And one is enough to re-create the entire universe.

But a re-creation of the universe is another way of looking at a mythic program or plan.

No one can tell us what the universe is but we may have any number of personal re-creations of it.

One exquisite datum then suffices for a re-creation of the universe if it is accepted by a person.

"But what is a person? You or I must take full responsibility for it, from inception through evolution to consummation. This will turn me or you into a person and make you more of a person. You can say that you are someone as soon as you have seen at least one mythic program or plan through to the end. You will be someone to be reckoned with and your speech will carry weight."

"And why not until then?"

"You wonder at this? Consider that no two persons are exactly alike, but that all people are exactly alike. As a person among others you will have nothing to gain except if the difference you make is your own. Not as a human being now, but as a person. People never make any difference except en masse, and then only in a totally mechanical fashion, where one thing must lead to the same thing without fail. But for a human being to divest itself of its individuality, in which all human beings are equal, and become a person, wherein all human beings are different, it must invest its individuality, that part of it which seems unwilling to change, in a universal transformation, so that all of it is changed."

"Universal transformation? That sounds cheap."

"Think about it. If all of you is changed, according to one single factor, the one we initially called an exquisite datum when you took it for granted as an external seal on your achieved perfection – and remember that this is a science, the one we call mythology – would it not have to fall out that however we begin, formed this way or that way, in love with our existence or inclined towards death, temperamentally deluded by a popular fiction or sexually distraught with our blame fixed to an object, eventually what we knew ourselves to be would have had to give way to what we are as knowledge; would have had to make room for what we become as love, since love and knowledge are the main-springs of our eternal personality, both origin and source of it?"

But you mentioned making a difference. What is it in me that urges me to come out of myself and make a difference, and why can I not leave things be?"

"What urges you is your individuality. You make a difference incidentally, you do not set out to do so. When you do set out to do so, you raise your individuality, to pick up your cross and go in a certain direction, to invest your individuality in a higher form of life, and this is where the term evolution comes in very handy. You have heard of Mr. Darwin's concept of mechanical evolution?"

"I have."

"And have you been able to make any headway with it? Has it helped you to increase your understanding, your ability to love?"

"I am afraid not. But I have always put that down to my being rather slow-witted."

"Would you prefer to be quick-witted?"

Here the master in me turned to the pupil in me and smiled encouragement .

"1 certainly would. I prefer joy to sadness too."

"And would you prefer life to a nondescript sort of existence where nothing much bothers you and nothing much matters to you except other people's regard? I have to ask this question, you see, because there are those who do not believe that any such thing is possible, as what I call life here, and they have washed their hands of it long ago. So we ought to consider that first, otherwise, if we neglect our foundation, we will end up talking in circles and agreeing on platitudes. You do then agree that there is something called life which is worth striving for, at first, and then later on, much more easily, gathering it in. And is it more important for you to live than to be seen to be living?"

"I think I know what you mean. Yes, it certainly is."

"Then you would better turn quite resolutely away from all these so-called studies and disciplines whose sole purpose it is to prove and make palatable the contention that the mechanical existence is all we have and that nothing greater is available for anyone. Some people dedicate years, often their entire existence to this task. They interpret the past and everything they can lay their hands on in the pale fluorescent glow of an extinct vision of things."

"That sounds terrible. What should our attitude be towards those people, if indeed they go about their business as you describe it – and I do harbour some reservations, you don't mind if I admit this to you. Should we not be outraged and strive against them in order to overcome their falsehoods and their mischief?"

"But you see, considering the nature of the thing we talk about, human existence itself and the life to be gained, that is quite impossible. You might as well try to drain a quicksand by walking through it. The only way to cope on such an occasion is to watch out for it carefully and when you notice it you must avoid it. Simply turn way from it and walk in another direction."

"And that other direction is a kind of transformation of oneself?"

"I would like to get back to my own use of the term 'evolution' if you don't mind."

"Ah yes, we strayed away from that, didn't we."

"Perhaps you can recall how a little while ago, when our master-pupil relationship was not yet very firmly established, we spoke about the inception of a divine element – "

"An exquisite datum, yes, I remember – "

"Well, can you tell what has happened in the meantime?"

"You might say that you and I have come into being."

"But now tell me this, if you can, because I would really like to know: did we come into being because of something we did, you and I, or was it done for us; was the way prepared for us, for our coming into being."

"The latter, I should think. Yes definitely."

"And who did this for us, are we able to know that? Or do we have to remain ignorant with respect to that particular knowledge? At the moment I am not sure; please tell me how you feel about this."

"I feel embarrassed about it, to say the least."

" Embarrassed! Well, I am certainly glad you can admit that to me. But let me pry a little further. I hope you don't think I am being less than personal. You and I should always do our best to be as one person to another, each complete in his own search for knowledge and understanding."

"I know what you mean."

"Then what about this embarrassment? Are we not dealing with facts, simply and plainly?"

"Evidently not."

"I agree. There seems to be more to it than facts; not that we should ever be of two minds about the value of facts. Without them, what would little boys do, eh, as the popular song goes? But what else? I too feel the embarrassment. Are we afraid to admit something to each other? There is nothing that is secret that will not be revealed, I am quite confident of that."

"That I should have to thank someone else for what is most precious to me: my being – perhaps that's it. It may turn out that I am not entirely a self-made person."

"Ah."

"I know how the story goes, or at least one of them, that god created man out of – whatever it was; I have no quarrel with that.

"You don't feel embarrassed about that?"

"Indeed no. As a human being, so it seems, at the moment at any rate, I feel quite comfortable and alright, being tied by an umbilical cord, to a natural, a universal womb. It conforms to my picture of all human beings. Even people have ..."

"But do continue with the other."

"Yes, the other. As a person I have always felt rather proud of my independence. But that was before I came into this being as you call it. Now it seems that I have a struggle on my hands."

"Let me help you. What kind of a struggle is it?"

"Well, I certainly prefer the truth of this being. I do feel that I belong here, really and truly. But the logical implications, as you pointed them out, bother me. Shall I call it a question of good taste? I have been taught to admire that a man makes his own decisions and chooses according to his own conscience and sense of responsibility, in all matters of existence and life. Now it appears that if I want this very highest and greatest and most glorious existence and life, once having come into being, I shall have to involve someone else in it, and admit that someone else is included in it, right from the start. How repulsive! How utterly dishonourable! – I come right out with it, to let you know how I feel."

"I am glad you can do that."

"And it seems to be someone like myself. Not very heroic or popular at all."

"How can you tell?"

"Because he makes no claims for himself and insists on nothing. He leaves it entirely up to me. He makes no demands, enters into no bargains or contracts, leaves me free to accept or reject him, threatens me with no punishment if I ignore him. But I know this, to my shame, that if I go back to my independent humanity I shall have to give up what I have learned to value most about myself, which is the fact that I have life, personal life, fresh, not second hand, clean above all, especially in my feeling and conscience. I am aware of being someone. But ..."

"But what?"

"Someone else was here first. You said so yourself. We could not even have come into this being if it had not been for him."

"But why should that worry us? When a captain means to take his ship into a new port, is he ashamed to take on a pilot? Someone who knows the reefs and the currents?"

"Oh dear, that sounds too traditional for my liking. I mean no disrespect, but those allegories have almost taken on a substitute life of their own these days. In my opinion they have become more of a hindrance than a help."

"I wonder, would that be so because they are allegories or because they have become linked exclusively to a traditionalist critique, sometimes domineering, sometimes shame-faced. I really can't say for sure. But maybe we can get around this difficulty some other way. You do after all come to me sometimes with these burning questions in your heart and the best I can do is help you find the answer there too, in your own heart, at the very place where the question arose, at the source of the problem in yourself. And I have noticed numerous times that in order to be successful in this I must continue to clear my mind of all prejudice and my body of all inhibition, so that I can love you straight and with a purpose, not afraid of being timid, feeble or weak."

"Is it always important for a teacher to love his pupil?"

"Absolutely crucial."

"Then show me by all means how this life I want and crave, this very specific and wondrous life, can spring from my own heart and I don't have to feel ashamed of it. If you can do that, I will truly call you my master."

"Ah, pardon me, we might as well start there. I have no interest in being called master by anyone. The only reward I want is that you succeed in your ambition. I would not want you to be grateful or ungrateful to me. And do not think I am being generous or altruistic. I know what I want. I would much rather be your friend than your master. As a matter of fact, now that I think about it, my being your master is quite out of the question. But now explain to me how you picture this life you have in mind, and perhaps we can take it from there."

"Ah, how I picture it! It goes on forever, first of all, that seems to be extremely important, and I would feel quite disappointed, cheated actually, if someone were to persuade me that eventually it came to nothing. Mind you, right away, even as I talk to you..."

"Yes?"

"I realize that there are no words to express what I fear. It seems that I can say quite successfully what this life is, that it goes on forever, for example, and that if it stopped it would have to start again, but when it comes to describing the opposite I cannot make sense. I mentioned that eventually it might come to nothing, but then it would carry on in fact, would it not? So I have a problem here – which really is no problem."

"We should all have such problems! They say that a mystic cannot say what is most dear to him. With you it seems to be the other way around. You cannot say what is opposite to what you value."

"Perhaps because it has no opposite. And you have to be in it to know it. So once you know it, your language takes on a new meaning. It opposes nothing but simply swallows it up. Fundamentally it praises, I suppose, and everything else follows from that."

"I must say you are becoming very articulate. Do you speak from the heart?"

"Where no contradiction may abide, eh? Is that how a poet puts it?"

"That is how you put it."

"Then you have led me around to where I have answered my own question. How clever of you. I couldn't have done it without you."

"So there we have common ground; I mean with our previous view of things. Does it embarrass you or make you feel in any way ashamed to realize that you needed me?"

"I see what you mean. No, strangely enough it does not."

"But you were not able to make your choices independently from me; you needed me to help you make them."

"Quite true. I wonder why I feel quite alright about that, but not about the other."

"Shall I tell you? I believe I know."

"Try, please, but take it slowly. A lot seems to be at stake here."

"The life you mean can be visible or invisible. When you agree to make use of me to make your choices, that life is invisible and in your case that makes matters plain, and you don't feel threatened or challenged. You realize, surely enough, that there is more to it than myself alone and that the willing dependence is what matters, yours on me and of course mine on you, but since you cannot picture it, this willing dependence, you are not affronted by it – equating for the moment visibility with picturability, I hope you don't mind."

"Not at the moment."

"Good for you. Then we both have a sense of humour."

"But when I look back now to our previous case, to the one that caused me some emotional difficulty, so that I felt like rejecting the help I had undoubtedly required ..."

"We had required ..."

"Yes, quite ... I can only see the one crucial difference – when I compare the two."

"And what is that?"

"Then it had been done in the past. Now, the other time, we do it in the present. When I look back, I begin to picture it, and the life becomes visible. I imagine it, personally. Right now there seems to be no need to imagine it, so it remains invisible. And the personal aspect of it causes me no problems."

"Suddenly we have discovered a great deal that could be talked about and we would do well to limit ourselves to two or three related points. I am of the opinion that you and I mean the same when we say life, and you would probably agree with me that our main reason for the present discussion is so that we may have this life. So let me review the situation we find ourselves in at the moment. We mentioned earlier that you and I could not even have come into being, as live human beings, if someone had not prepared the way for us; you agreed with this but confessed to a sense of shame, possibly even guilt, certainly embarrassment, as soon as you contemplated the necessary truth of that matter. We then discovered that right here and now you have it in your heart to accept totally our dependence on one another for this eternal life, and that you experienced no sense of unease at all when you approached it in the present, in the light of day as it were. You then chose to wonder, remarkably enough, why this might be so, and I explained it in terms of your personal inclination for accepting this life, your live being, invisibly, and in terms of your disinclination to give your heart to it, to accept it emotionally, as soon as it appeared, visibly, imagined or pictured. Do you agree with my résumé so far?"

"Yes, definitely."

"Then would you let me go on to point something out to you which has, I believe, an important bearing on what we are discussing? I warn you that you may not find it pleasant to hear."

"Tell me nevertheless, please. You have shown me in the past how a great deal of worthwhile knowledge introduces itself painfully."

"Very well, I can see that you intend to understand what I have to say and that you do not mean to quarrel with me. Do you recall when earlier you asked whether it is always important for a teacher to love his pupil and I answered: absolutely crucial?"

"Yes, I do."

"And then you said: 'Then show me by all means how this life I want and crave, this very specific and wondrous life, can spring from my own heart and I don't have to feel ashamed of it. If you can do that, I will truly call you my master.'"

"Yes, I can recall saying that. But why do you repeat it to me?"

"Because I would like you to know how it embarrassed me to hear you say that, and how I felt for a moment that you had insulted my intelligence. I was ashamed for you."

"Oh dear!"

"So can you fathom the implication?"

"Not really. I am slightly shocked at the moment."

"The implication seems to be that we either bear the shame of our lesser life ourselves or else we ask someone else to bear it for us. (By lesser life I mean our life at a certain given point in time in comparison to the life to come, to the life we are about to appropriate or grow into. And while eternal life cannot be comprehended materially and mechanically, it is however substantial, so that a comparison of it in time makes sense. So while you spoke straight from your beautiful heart, you did not realize how much of a demand you were making on me, how far you presumed on my love. It took a great deal of love for me to point out to you that the master you were looking for just then was not … ah, but I did make a poor job of it all the same, so far as I can recall. Pardon me while I hide my face. "

"But you guided me back in the right direction all the same, I can see that now. Secretly I wanted you to lie to me, so that I could make an oracle of my own heart. I myself wanted to be that oracle. I am grateful to you for preventing me. As for the shame you felt, that sets me to thinking now. If I naturally incline towards the life as invisible, how often will I risk indulging my self and compromising someone else, presuming on someone else's love, as you put it so succinctly. And shall I choose to go against my inclinations? For you have helped me to know myself ."

"Either way one runs a risk. You tend to overestimate your feeling and you seem to forget that the responsibility for forces unleashed that way must eventually be taken by someone, someone else if not yourself right from the start. In my own case one might speak of a superabundance of reflection. Unless I am very, very careful I prove my point to the satisfaction of everyone but myself ."

"You prefer the life as visible?"

"Yes I do. I do indeed."

"And I suppose it would occur to you then rather too readily to criticize anyone who lacks an identifiable justification for his existence."

"You have put your finger on the spot."

"You sometimes sacrifice the content to the form, the picture to the frame, in order to domineer over a distance."

"How well you know me."

"It seems that neither one of us has much to crow about."

"Not when it comes down to our just deserts."

"But what a marvellous institution is friendship! Here we can reveal our faults and shortcomings to each other, and we can discuss ways of avoiding and overcoming them. We can love one another in spite of our mistakes, without being critical."

"Yes, I agree. Whole-heartedly. Friendship is more important than any conviction based on opinion. And I would consider it to be quite an achievement if a pupil and a teacher could eventually become friends."

"I accept your challenge."

"But what do we say to those who would persuade us that true friendship is humanly impossible, in short, that it is a myth?"

"We might try to explain to them the difference between friendship as a myth and friendship as myth. In that way we would find our way back to our common origin as scientific inventions. What do you say to that?"

"Agreed. Let us dedicate the rest of our existence to myth as friendship."

*

Myth as friendship:

Would you tell a friend the truth at the risk of making him your enemy? Or would you dispense with truth in the interest of tying your friend more closely to yourself?

We would go so far as to say that friendship, as an activity and as something that is done, must not only preserve but actually seek to increase the friend's personal freedom.

But personal freedom is not freedom from one thing or another, but it is freedom to grow and freedom for growth.

While I help someone primarily to free himself from falsehood, even from my own falsehood, I cannot yet call him my friend. Conversely, the direct influence I have on someone's personality in the interest of the enrichment and nourishment of that personality, granted that such a thing is possible, should definitely be called friendship.

This excludes, or rather does not include, the concept of reciprocity. I can be someone's friend and that person does not know about it and he may forever remain unaware of it. So often association is taken for friendship. But association is reciprocal. And I do not mean 'mere' association.

Now two things can be seen to be important if I would be someone's friend and if I would offer him friendship: I must be more aware of what is good for that person than that person is and in addition to this I must choose to apply my greater awareness to the benefit of that person.

Since we are dealing with spiritual values here, one person's benefit cannot imply another person's disadvantage, such as may be the case with money, where more of it for you may mean less for me, but in reality whatever is to your advantage must also be to my advantage, and whatever benefits me must also benefit you. The fact that I can seek my own advantage most successfully by working to yours is a definition of life.

Up to here we have said nothing about friendship that cannot be duplicated on a rational plane. It applies readily to that realm of thought and emotion which we have elsewhere called modern and which is characterized by a discrepancy between mutually inclusive opposites, such as man – God , where God is pictured as condescending to man and saving him, depending on man's willingness, or man is pictured as striving to see God and becoming one with Him, depending on God's willingness. Neither God without man nor man without God makes much sense, and this we call the mutual inclusiveness of the relationship, but at the same time God and man are opposite; human and divine are experienced as categories while theoretically they have to be manipulated as terms or put into action as concepts before they can be said to be relevant, and in order for the relation to be maintained, the discrepancy must be preserved. Either a state of tension is kept up or extinction sets in. Rest cannot be attained in concrete terms but has to be hoped for 'beyond the grave' while 'on this side' it implies a falling away and a sliding back. The modern relation extends to all walks of life, including life and death itself, but more specifically to man and woman, husband and wife, parent and child, ruler and subject, observer and object, eye and environment, world and spirit, creature and creator, you and I, the individual and society, and so on indefinitely; it does not extend, for our present purpose, to friend and friend, where we intend to demonstrate one incident of emergence from the modern era.

A trait that signals the modern relationship for us is that one member of the duality is dominant and the other recessive. A type of tension is created by insistence on one or the other as dominant or recessive. Schools are encouraged to come into being to argue against inheritance as the dominant factor in the case of evolution, others argue for it and against environment, so that when the origin of present characteristics is analyzed, a primary tension is created by dividing the field into inheritance and environment and a secondary tension is manufactured between those who lean to the view that inheritance plays the dominant role and environment the recessive one and those who prefer that inheritance should recede and the environment dominate. The view that both play an equal role leads to extinction. While the tension is fed, progress is made.

In order to make the modern era comprehensible, particular cases have to be cited, because only from outside the modern era, in emergence from it perhaps, can we see it distinctly.

Another instance that would help to illustrate the modern relationship might be the duality of Church and State at the time of Constantine the Great and the way minds were, and still are, divided on issues such as the recession of the Church since its worldly institution or the domination of the Church since then; or the decline of the Roman State since its compromise with the Roman Church, or the developing sovereignty of the HRE since the fertilizing influence of the Church on the State.

The point to be made emphatically is that a contemporary emergence from the modern era into the light of day is not to be achieved by way of harmonious anodynes, such as World Councils or Unified Field Theories, nor is it to be managed by a one-sided, extremist push such as a personality cult, nationalism or the mechanization of morals.

One way for this emergence to succeed however is by way of mythology, which is knowledge for the understanding of myth, and in the present case of myth as friendship.

*

Myth as friendship is an act of love superimposed.

It makes no sense to ask: superimposed on what, precisely because the superimposition would not be required if we knew *on what*. Whether or not we are capable of such an act of friendship depends entirely on our understanding of myth and on our knowledge of its availability to us at a particular time. Because myth is involved, first of all, the present moment is of the essence. Whether or not we actually perform such an act of love as this friendship however depends entirely on our willingness to respond to a judged set of human circumstances, and this will have to be discussed at length. We cannot go into detail about the particularity or eventuality of such circumstances because these can once again only be determined in the past, as part of the historic past, made historic in fact by our act of love superimposed, but we can go to some length about what we mean by a judged set of human circumstances, to which we respond willingly in friendship or with which we refuse to have anything to do for one reason or another, and none of these reasons can be foretold.

A judged set of circumstances occurs in the case of an individual person. If we ask now how someone can be individual and a person at the same time we arrive at the crux of the matter. The two at the same time are out of the question, since individuality pertains to mental time, to time that is conceived of as measured in hours by clocks and in years by the calendar and nothing beyond that, so that our individuality, whenever it occurs, always has to be temperamental, while personality implies time that is properly experienced, to which we refer as eternal time, which does not exclude clock and calendar time, or temporal time, but it renders such time serviceable. In the case of an individual temperament (or of a temperamental individual) temporal time is not serviceable but either empirical or imperious, depending on whether the individuality is controlled or in control. Individuality in control terrifies, as we know all too well, and this excessive knowledge, as we go beyond the bounds of personality, leads to terrorism, where the conventions are misunderstood and traditions are abused. There is no way back for the terrorist but only to be cut off. Controlled individuality, by comparison, builds up to an unbearable burden of pressure due to an internal or psychic contradiction, an

opposition of forces that can neither be sustained nor re-
solved and so must lead to catastrophe or end in tragedy.
Of course we all know how we tend to control our individuality allegedly so that it will not get into control and
us under its control, when in fact we merely delight in the
relative sense of power that comes, as a feeling, with
self-sustained and self-inflicted pressures and arrogant
pride; or how we lean to our individuality for guidance,
and we like to do this, to submit to its control, putatively
to lend force to our conviction and violence to our persuasion, within or without, but actually for no other reason than that we prefer to feel driven and that we like to
drift, because it deadens our conscience and kills our
sense of responsibility.

Since an individual person at a time, or at one time,
cannot be, it must be an illusion, and to say that something is an illusion implies a dual character and a double
identity, in short, a division against itself but in such a
way that service may be given and enlightenment created. In order to accentuate this aspect of an illusion, we
compare it to a delusion, when our functions are inca-
pacitated and our faculties are duped.

Illusion operates as history and works as nature. An illusion, however, such as an individual person as such,
operates as history or works as nature, and never the two
at once. For an individual person there can be no peace
and there is no rest. The Son of Man has nowhere to lay
his head. The thing we call friendship, and which we describe in terms of myth as friendship and define as an act
of love superimposed upon a judged set of human circumstances, turns an individual person towards manhood

or womanhood, so that by choice that particular person may put his individuality at the service of his humanity, even to the extent of its entire subsummation under humanity as a human being and to the point of consummation as a man or a woman. We notice the evolution of character and the development of personality here towards manhood or womanhood, and we especially take stock of the fact that our individuality is put to use and not either glorified or sacrificed, as the modern world would have it. If we would emerge from modernity into the light of the present day, we must take some pains first to acknowledge this fact of our individuality as either dispensable or triumphant, an acknowledgment that may take the form of admission or confession, and then to put it to good use. The employment and investment of our individuality more specifically makes for humanity and for human being.

History and nature are seen and experienced by an individual person as somehow in mutual counterproductivity. In other words, whatever is deemed to be natural is so at the expense of history to some extent, and equally whatever is considered to be historical takes away somehow from nature to some degree.

We are typifying a set of human circumstances here insofar as it is judged.

There are the products of history and the products of nature. For the individual person, judged as an individual person and so rendered for a time indefinite, as we all experience during our moments of crisis, in anxiety or doubt, in panic or terror, in short in extremity; for such an individual person each and every product of history seems to tempt him to an ultimate identification of his self or his ego with some image of immortality, with some picture of time not as a temporary, measured thing, but as an endless series of events, and so, consequently, instead of memory being stimulated and the past being illustrated, there is a confusion of fact with fable, of definition with information, and regretfully a story, a perfectly good story even, is taken for 'nothing but' a story and dismissed. But any product of history, any relation of what happened, contains, due to this relation, a contemporary source of imagination, and those who mistake the story for 'nothing but' a story cut themselves off from this source and to that extent incur impoverishment. To relate what happened means basically to turn past time into imagination. This turn, however, so fundamental to our easy existence itself, is either defeated due to a childish gullibility or else forestalled on account of a skeptical criticism. In either direction, the relation is made impossible. The gullible ones cry: 'We have played with you and you won't let us win,' while the critics maintain: 'We won't let you play with us because we might lose.' Typical products of history are creation stories, such as Adam and Eve in paradise.

An imaginative product of history is the virgin birth of Jesus. Spiritual products of history are the parables told by Jesus as reported by apostles. Critical products of history are the dialogues of Plato. Fantastic products of history are novels by Thomas Mann. Superficial (not merely superficial) products of history are the productions of journalism. A trivial (not nothing but trivial) production of history might be the diffident reminiscence of an individual person in the seat next to you on the train tomorrow morning.

In all of these cases only one thing matters: whether we make use of the product or not. If we do not, nothing is lost, but if we are critical or gullible a great deal is lost.

Keep in mind the crucial difference between being critical or indulging in criticism and doing something critically or practicing critique. The same thing goes for the difference between gullibility or indulging oneself in credulity and doing something credibly or giving credit. The one thing that encompasses both critique and credit we call belief, and what we do when we really believe, neither blindly nor surreptitiously, makes proper use of the products of history. Belief volunteers trust and does not require evidence, as we do in the case of the products of nature, but applies a person directly and immediately to time.

Now I know that it seems as though we were banishing history to the East and nature to the West and never the twain shall meet, but this is not the case. We are not undertaking an academic study but performing an act of friendship, which means separating, at the moment, what is joined wrongly and then allowing it to join up correctly. Before we can expect a child to put on shoes properly we have to show him how the left shoe differs from the right shoe, and only then can the shoes be worn as a pair. We have defined an individual person as someone whose shoes often pinch because of a confused notion about history and nature when in life these two make a pair.

We turn now to the products of nature and discover that here too, insofar as these become part of a judged set

144

of human circumstances, they are seen in conflict with history and experienced in some manner as opposed to its products, being more trustworthy and reliable, lending themselves less readily to truth and imagination, whichever way one's bias misleads.

Now just as the individual person, this illusion who is neither totally individual, delusion, nor completely a person, reality – just as such an individual person is tempted to identify with the products of history, so is that person tried by the products of nature. (We should mention here, by the way, that an individual is the same delusion as a personality. If I insist that I know, I delude myself and become an individual, a delusion, and if others insist that I know and I fall in with their opinions of me I am deluded and become a personality.)

The products of nature try us and become a trial to us when we do not take them at face value but endow them with a superior set of values which they in themselves cannot support. Then, when they disappoint us, we reject them out of hand.

Products of nature are always complete in themselves, however. They do not allow us to interpret them partially, not because they resent us or because of some material truculence which needs to be overcome, nor on account of a stubborn refusal to comply with our wishes, but because they must be wholly accepted or not at all. 'Welcome the one who comes in the name of the lord.' Interpretation is out of place and the partial approach only makes matters worse.

Now in addition to this, we have to stress the fact for the time being that products of nature are not believed, like products of history, but known. Knowledge applies to them. Knowledge also is acquired from them. Similarly we can say that we gain knowledge from products of nature by applying our senses to them. And at the same time knowledge is an accumulation of sense which we call our body.

As soon as we know our body now, once we have one, we become capable of natural products ourselves, such as this science. Our own body gives evidence which we take into account and on which we base our understanding, and whatever we refer to our body, as vision or as experience, may be known through that medium of vision or experience, and whatever we can not refer to our body is none of our business and does not concern us.

But the evidence and testimony due to our body on account of vision and experience is never made public and does not remain private but is always open and available to all, as a stimulus to vitality and as a source of refreshment. Our works are not published but they are handed down and around. We may certainly make an effort with respect to those who may benefit from our works, but we have nothing to gain from such an effort.

And as soon as our body makes do with the products of nature, our mind is satisfied with the products of history, so that between knowledge and belief we have life in abundance and plenty. A judged set of human circumstances, in comparison to this, first pales into insignificance, where individuality is obstructed, and then becomes self-contradictory, so that personality becomes problematic. In friendship we see this and act.

An act of friendship limits itself to a single instance of humanity in order to render it relevant to the light of day. Myth as friendship touches the individual person at the time when individuality is not significant but receptive and when the personality is problematic but self-conscious. Love at that moment is substantially instilled. It begins to make a difference now in a sense and for a time, radically and urgently, and then it either bears fruit, in an act of love again though not necessarily friendship, or else it manifests itself as contemplative awareness.

*

An act of love

And yet, while all these passing pains
explore my cold heart, causing grief,
quick memory, based on love, explains
what use are knowledge and belief.

You search within, I find without,
and both have purpose more than ought,
nor may each one bring love about
where spirit fires what sense has brought.

If we but wait, though charm hold fire
until the passing of the moon,
what little time our hearts require
to heal as one will find us soon.

This room lends comfort to our cares,
this house supports the love we feel,
and yet, while Christ's sword spurns or spares
our world, this life can not be real.

*

Contemplative awareness implies something to contemplate but it should not be confused with a contemplating awareness, where a leading light is followed.

Awareness as such allows for no difference or discrepancy between inner and outer, between visible and invisible, but it encompasses them both. If usually we discriminate between the realm of the spirit and material things, between flesh and spirit, here we refrain from doing this and concentrate instead on our human being with respect to everything else indiscriminately. We cannot concentrate on our human being in itself since that would imply a contradiction, considering that humanity is the essence of all being, but with respect to everything else my humanity – since I am a human being and a person, in particular the person presently communicating with you – becomes concentric while everything else becomes cosmic.

These become, they are not, so there must be an outcome or an issue, and this we call the mythic product, or, which is the same, the product of myth, which is to say: myth as a product.

*

Myth as a product:

We have mentioned products of history and products of nature, and by the way, it helps to define what we mean by myth as a product when we just point out how a natural product is not the same as a product of nature and an historic product is not the same as a product of history, but a mythic product and a product of myth, or myth as a product – these can be used interchangeably without doing violence.

Contemplative awareness, we have said, issues in myth as a product. Only a fully fledged human being is capable of such awareness, and only a complete person, or rather a perfect person, actually does it, because a prerequisite for it is a fully invested individuality.

Now the proper word that describes the investment of our individuality is care. Compare this to charisma, which is individuality disguised as spirit, or fake personality, and to popularity, which is individuality as a myth, or as a lie. Care is definitely to be preferred, because it does us good, rather than harm, like the others.

A careful investment of what we are like then starts the process. We study how we tend to behave, what our usual reactions are, under what circumstances we lose our temper or go into an emotional slump, not in order to make an inventory, however, or so as to draw up a profile of ourselves that might interest others, but strictly for the sake of scientific prediction.

Scientific prediction of individual selves, loosely called knowledge of ourselves, makes for the main aspect of individuality investment.

But now we have to make one thing clear first. When we refuse to invest our individuality and instead try to make it stand on its own two feet or attempt to let it be something in itself, this individuality is a negativity. It becomes very boring, or it crumbles after a show of strength, or it behaves in a beastly fashion, straight over a cliff, or it surrounds itself with an aura of respectability and righteousness, eventually to go up in a puff of smoke. When we build on our individuality we build on proverbial sand.

Insofar as I insist on my individuality, usually as my right or as my bargain piece to get me into the social contract, I think of myself as unique and as ever so interesting, in short as one of a kind, who deserves to be celebrated and tends to be overlooked. Human beings will tolerate me and bear with me for a while and they will ask themselves and each other the following questions about me: Is it a lost cause? should we hope for a change of heart? will love effect anything here at the moment?

Do we need to protect ourselves? Do we notice any lasting change in response to our trust?

So I refer to my self at my peril, because ten to one I will also be referring to your self and probably you will not thank me for it, the point being that your self and my self are indistinguishable. We cannot compare them because they are not there to be compared, and any attempt to compare them makes both of us fall back, unless at least one of us is mercifully constituted; we will try to come back later to this extraordinarily important reality of a merciful constitution which can turn even selfishness into its opposite. For or the moment let us remain with the inalienable right of an individual to destroy all individuality, either by insisting on it or by refusing to countenance it.

Of course as soon as I even mention my individuality, I must be aware or at least conscious of it to some degree, unless I am talking nonsense, and to that degree I am ahead of the individual who simply does not know; who is a simpleton or an ass, say, or generally what we call a fool. To suffer such a fool gladly is then the only profitable course left to us. And we know fools by their total blindness to the fact that they are individual.

Such a rock-bottom individuality likes to run together in herds and to indulge itself in mass movements, and the greater the number of individuals that agree or come together on something, the smaller the individual or singular consciousness of individuality that would mean a possible move towards integrity as a person. The eventual annihilation of a fool or of a mass of fools is a pleonasm because the foolishness of unconscious individuality is already what we mean by extinction and annihilation. More precisely we call a successful insistence on individuality extinction, while annihilation is the term we reserve for unconscious individuality or outright foolishness.

So much for that. Extinction and annihilation are islands and blank walls. What interests us now is everything that tends away from these and approaches integrity, personality and finally a merciful constitution, which could be viewed as the positive pole opposite one's negative self.

I notice in my own self, for example, something terribly attractive, but only insofar as I seem to be able to sum up very nicely something totally negative there. And the attraction decreases and eventually disappears as soon as I give my full attention to it. This was not always so. Because my own self, not I, by the way, is in the end instinctive. Part of my individuality is involved in my instincts or, in another way, I am to some extent instinctual. Like any aspect of my individuality, this works against me unless I take account of it and make myself responsible for it.

151

The last bit of one's individuality to be invested – in my own case the instinctive bit – is always the most difficult, it seems, probably because one fears that then one has no more excuses to fall back on, but even this last bit can be included, and this is where mercy comes in. Not only is it required if we mean to complete the job in hand, but in order for the job to remain done and not to become repeatedly undone we must become capable of mercy and we must practice it.

Where mercy is required we depend on belief and where we become capable of mercy we depend on knowledge, but the actual practice of mercy involves myth.

Let us go back for the moment to that remnant of individuality, residual instinct in my case, so that we may track mercy to its foundation. Because here, buried deep in our organic make-up, we come across the very roots of our being; and now we have to decide whether everything that is rooted here pertains to our being, and we may come to the conclusion that some of it does not, and we may even feel urged to uproot whatever does not pertain to our being or we may feel driven to eradicate everything that smacks in the least of an organic connection or source; and yet we would be so wrong to do this, because the harm is always greater than the benefit.

The realm of our organic make-up is a fact and there is no getting around it. We are organized beings prior to our existence as human beings. This is a hopeful state, so that the organized being need not despair, saying: I am not a human being; but rather: I am not a human being yet.

On the other hand, a human being is ill-conceived inorganically and would tend to the demonic or the angelic, and this is why we spoil our chances of humanity to the extent that we cut ourselves off from our organic being.

We have a right to call it _our_ organic being, by the way, while we accept or choose it as part and parcel of our human being and while we view human being correctly, as partly organic. However while we try to cut ourselves off from it, there cannot be any organic being for us and what usually happens is that we consider ourselves as supersophisticated and extremely civilized while in fact we have turned into organisms. On the other hand, if instead of cutting ourselves off from it we go to the other extreme and organize our existence with the aid of extinct institutions, so that we avoid the light of day, and we do this in order to avoid the light, we again have no organic being, but this time because we have no being, having become extinct.

We must admit at this point that from the standpoint of myth there is neither opposition nor conflict between our organic make-up and our human being, and in addition to this we should confess that any discrepancy between the two is always for the sake of a mythic product, so that eventually we do well to welcome any such discrepancy because it puts myth productively within our grasp.

From admission through confession to the final welcome there is a path of human evolution that deserves to be followed up in detail. However for the time being we intend to busy ourselves with an analysis of the merciful constitution of organic humanity in comparison to its sacrifice, insofar as this can be done.

Only once we have decided finally to say no to human sacrifice, even in its organic form, in favour of our merciful constitution, can we see clearly and understand thoroughly what a waste of resources is implied by an insistence on sacrifice and how in fact this greatest of all human developments in a world community cannot even be approached while we still hanker, even spuriously, after a mechanical influence, on our environment or by our environment, of our God or by our God. An analysis of sacrifice as such would take us too far afield, especially since that term has undergone such a tremendous change in the individual consciousness, usually so as to avoid radical reform. Organized religion, especially by its more popular appeal, has encouraged such a widespread adoption of sacrifice at the very heart of human activity itself that frequently one can only turn away in horror from the murderous reality behind the benign mask. And where the fear of God and the respect for the Law join hands in this enterprise, no wonder the contemporary mind waxes apocalyptic!

So instead of an analysis of sacrifice, which could be managed completely but would take us disgracefully far beyond the confines of our present study, we choose to undertake a comparative and partial analysis of the merciful strain in the human organism, and this in order to demonstrate as cogently as lies in our power how the mythic product is feasible and why it should under any and all circumstances be encouraged and espoused.

Mercifully we take care even of what disagrees with us and of what we dislike.

A timid proposition like this announces, in its very timidity, that which seems often most likely to stimulate a merciful disposition in ourselves, as we have noticed most obviously during stressful situations and in keeping with our best interests while under the influence of a religious mood.

But a merciful disposition or a religious mood only approximates, in one practical form or another, for the contemplative faculty or to the awareness of the eye, what eventually may become, due to action and habit, on the basis of both being and becoming, an entirely changed nature for the good.

Nevertheless we must start somewhere .

A merciful disposition allows us to make headway with someone whose rebellious nature has shut him off from benign influence. A religious mood allows us to be influenced benignly where our nature would otherwise rebel and shut us off. So a merciful disposition involves a benign influence, and one of which we are aware, while a religious mood is penetrated by a benign influence, and one which we contemplate.

A religious mood stems from a partial approximation of our organic nature to our human nature, and we remember that all religion has to do with these two becoming one. The mood lets us know that a closeness exists, and due to our understanding of moods in general we may now decide to go ahead and utilize this mood so as to render the closeness actual and lively. The mood is an operand. It is a sign of something and an opportunity for something. Religious moods are innumerable. It makes no difference where I detect them, in you or in myself, I can take advantage of them all the same and put them to good use. Elsewhere I have defined religion itself as knowledge for the sake of understanding moods, but here we have to do only with those moods which have already been understood, and our reason for exposing them is so that our humanity may be made organically permanent. We intend to build on rock.

But we may expose these moods in two ways, or rather in a way or in a manner, as an exposition or as an exposure. The exposure presents itself as a possibility and the exposition as a reality. We will pick the manner if we want to be pitied and we will choose the way if we want to grow. If we seek pity we may well throw light on an injustice but we do nothing to alleviate it. We only pass on the blame. But the exposition of a religious mood does away with the encumbrance which prevented the organic humanity prior to the mood, because we exhibit the burden we experience not to someone else or to a public institution or under private solicitation, professionally, vicariously or in partnership, but we exhibit it mythically.

The exposition of a religious mood is a mythic exhibition.

We don't make a scene and complain a lot and we do not try to make anyone feel bad by showing how much we have been hurt by them, nor do we cherish our pain as martyrs. Instead we welcome the opportunity to deepen our roots and then we take it. The burden is admitted, the weight is confessed, the solid is welcome so much in physical terms .

The exhibition is mythic, for example, insofar as we avoid inward or outward subjectivity or objectivity but relate instead. We do not criticize or become critical, for another example, but we obviate. The mythic aspect includes both the no and the yes. In other words, when we

156

call this exhibition mythic, we imply first of all a rejection of the exposure and then an espousal, the relation or the obviation of our two given examples. It makes no sense to ask: the relation of what? or: an obviation of what? because that would imply a state less than, or lower than, or other than mythic, while mythic states themselves do not even exist. On the other hand, whether relation or obviation or some other form of espousal, depends entirely on the nature of the exposition and on the particular religious mood which we exposed.

In the case of a mythic product, which is after all what we want to describe here, when we have done all we can, something happens to crown our efforts of knowledge and belief, and due to our merciful disposition we are able to direct right from the start the time and place of what happens rather than working in semi-darkness towards some unknown date. We described the direction in terms of obviation and relation, leaving the field open for others, but once the product exists, in the flesh (not as flesh, as in the case of exposure), we may then go ahead and describe it in the light of day, for general consumption, in colours or letters, in sounds, signs and gestures.

A merciful disposition now, in comparison to a religious mood as we have discussed it above, can be fostered by practice alone, as a readiness and a preparedness, for what will eventually come our way, either in ourselves or in others, as a recalcitrance before objective good, as an unwillingness to be guided by kindliness in the presence of people, by love in the company of human beings, by wisdom wherever individual persons approach us or leave us.

In order to make the real practical and everyday usefulness of a merciful disposition stand out more clearly, I intend to hold it next to that which seems to approximate to it most closely and yet remains miles apart from it, which is generally referred to as a mystical disposition.

For a mystical disposition prepares us for a solitary confinement of our happiness and pleasure, so that we mean to have these in secret even as we show others how to have them in secret. The disciplines of the mystic are really not disciplines at all but rigours which he forces himself to undergo on account of his manifold dispositions to an outward show.

This is why we can say that the mystic, like the critic, avoids his many errors by making a single mistake.

A merciful disposition may be cultivated, but this leaves us open to a certain degree of bigotry with disrespect shown to those whose expressions of mercy appear in a form different from ours, for cultivation implies a unity of method just as mysticism necessitates a unity of technique. So instead of cultivating a merciful disposition we do much better to practice mercy, always again and anew, even as the fluctuations of our temperament draw us off course or as the manifold face of our experience changes.

For with practice comes usage, in this too.

We do well not to cling to any customary type of behaviour, observing the hour and the day, but we return repeatedly to ourselves as mercifully disposed. We have done it once so we may do it again, and perhaps it helps us to keep in mind that we do not stand alone in our wish to remain mercifully inclined but that some came before us and are with us now.

In any case, if we study the matter more closely, we shall have to admit that a merciful disposition, viewed as such, is as much an act as it is a state or a condition, and that the mercy we have is the mercy we show or dispense. Again, this proves that we move presently in terms of communion, community and communication, where the found life is lost while the given life is gained, which can be clearly understood, but only while it is actually done too, not academically or in extinction. Because a merciful disposition is mythic in order, we may regard it from the side of action while we do it or we may act it out even as we describe it, but we realize all the time that it is not one or the other, action or condition, state or deed, one at the exclusion of the other, since the distinction between the two in this or any other case is after all made or maintained by us for a very specific purpose and does not reside in any reality or adhere to any truth.

As we suggested before, that which makes a mythic product such a precious commodity is that it holds sway.

So on one hand we are mercifully disposed, which derives from our being, while on the other hand we dispose ourselves mercifully, in response to some posture into which we have fled or been pushed for instance, or simply because our present position strikes us, on reflection, as in some way not merciful, in some manner merciless. Then too, on this other hand, where merciful disposition is viewed as an act, it may happen that we are being mercifully disposed by an agent or agency other than ourselves, and this is extremely difficult to take by some, especially those of us who have come all too much into the habit of insisting on doing for ourselves, as artists do, and consequently incline to the solitary confinement techniques of the mystic. Here purism and puritanism become risks and dangers. For when we are shown mercy and presently do not exist as mercifully disposed, we experience our own disorders as positioned or posited outside of ourselves and so we commit the injustice against mercy itself.

By purism or puritanism we try foolishly to protect ourselves against the scandal we both experience and cause in the face of external mercy.

Imagine someone who is always mercifully disposed or in a religious mood. No matter what else this person came up with in terms of thought and emotion, you could always count on a merciful disposition or on a religious mood, if not one then the other. If you yourself were incapable of mercy and had no ability for it, then this person's presence would always cause you to experience either rage or shame. You however, if worse came to worst, would blame that person and indulge yourself in accusations of evil of one sort or another. The least incident would serve you as a pretext for suspicion, superstition and jealousy. (Witness, as a dramatic example, the relationship of Desdemona and Othello.)

But mainly such a person would not feel remarkably attracted to you unless you too were capable of some specific and absolute reality, some perfect relation against which nothing could hold sway. Mercy, by way of operating more and more successfully, most naturally seeks reason as a partner, only at this level of the sound and inviolable function of course, so that we may well see reason and mercy grow up on each other, develop alongside and mature because of each other, merciful and reasonable being begetting merciful and reasonable persons.

A mythic product is a case of our being, of our human being, perfectly and naturally personified, or divinely instituted.

A divine institution of our being makes equal sense with a natural perfection of our humanity since god and man are one. Since then this is so, and we should make no apology for not right away understanding why for so long this has not been achieved. For not by achievement do we create what is, but rather we achieve what is, even so that it may become.

If this is not language as myth then nothing is, and we know it in terms of myth as language.

*

Myth as language:

We said previously that we would have to start somewhere when it came to the illustration of myth as a product and so we started with a merciful disposition and a religious mood because we felt that here lay the twin root and double source, source and origin, of myth in time. Any product makes time accessible to us, in some particular form, though a mythic product makes it accessible freely and substantially, and this we call eternal time, negatively viewed available as unproblematic.

Now while we take no offence at a source and an origin, we nevertheless search, as man has always searched,

161

for a single beginning, and there we arrive to our wonder and astonishment at an appreciation of myth as language. Not that language is seen as a product, but that in itself it produces, not this or that language, or even speech and writing, but myth pure and simple.

So myth as language is myth as produced by language, and we might as well come to the conclusion that we thrive or stumble by every word that issues from our mouths.

Mercy makes me mind my manners.

All these words sink or swim
In accordance with my best interests.

Reason rights the wronged heart
Each day anew, but an old man
Acquaints me with shameful extremes.

Dry seasons await, ice overpowers us
Where this recent secret is forgotten
Or laid at the feet of average men
Lost in admiration under ten stars.

Foolishly attempted we spring out and
Get hatred under way, as though momentary
Aches and pains saddled the gods with
Narrow minds and loose morals, or drew
Great sighs of relief from the breast.

Language we have and language we are and not one of these but both together make up for the wholeness of myth. However we cannot have language and be language both at the same time, which is a good thing, because from out of this impossibility all good things come to us. Neither can we have language all of the time or be language all of the time, but either for a time, and consequently we change, which serves us well, because out of this change comes our wellbeing.

All good things come to us out of the impossibility of being language and having language both at the same time, and this we call the good, or god. Goodness on the other hand is the name we give to that impossibility itself, and to the fact of it, because we know that these two, being language and having language, are both for us, and if they were possible both at the same time they could not be for us, so that we would be bad and things would be bad for us.

In contemplation of the flesh, goodness escapes us precisely on account of a seeming possibility of myth as one language. Not that the flesh is bad but the contemplation of it is maladroit. But the truth of the flesh as useless is difficult to bear while the truth of goodness as an impossibility is easy.

Now where we are addicted to the flesh we will immediately assume that the wise thing to do in the face of an impossibility is to turn away from it, and so we would turn away from goodness. But if we wait a moment and take the time to study this particular impossibility, we will come to see it rather as a boon and a blessing and we will take our definition of what in fact is possible from it, which is that we have language or are language, and then we will go ahead and either have it or be it, as we see fit, and so we know god.

Or again, we have language, say, and we have it until it runs over and then we can have it no more, which may strike us at first as an occasion for grief and sadness, but this would be wrong, because when what we have here runs over, this is the signal for us to be it. And then we change. And it is well for us to change, for we see the impracticality of continuing with what we had, and so we become what we had. We can say now that we are language, and we interpret our sadness and grief in such a way that we become language, so that to this extent we become responsible for our own wellbeing. This goes equally for persons as for mankind, which is why we undertook a comparative analysis.

Our past, as time past, whether we see it as a personal past or as mankind in the past, may again be contemplated as flesh, when the various appearances of events, whether accidental or planned, seem to hold a significance of their own which, however, must always be fleeting, or, instead of this, it may become part of our language today, of the language we are, and so be eternally past, which adds to our wellbeing, rather than taking away from it as when we try to make the past present, which is a damnable offence.

While we are language we limit ourselves, as I do now. We limit ourselves to such an extent that the language we are eventually turns into speech, and speech into communication. For speech in itself has nothing to do with communication, any more than language itself has anything to do with speech. Language itself might be defined as an interest we take in what goes on around us; the limitations of sound are required to turn it into speech. By the same token, speech in itself might be defined as the voice of god, but in order for this to become communication, the limitations of a human relationship are required, such as friendship or brotherhood.

But a personal relationship makes for the greatest communication and a limitation towards it is the most worthwhile.

So it would seem when humanity is seen as in its essence animal and the human being is contemplated as a complex of psychic forces in disarray for a time between birth and death. So it would seem but it is not.

So it is however when humanity is seen as in its essence divine. A personal relationship now is not extinct but live. But most important, as relevant to our present inquiry, personality is derived plainly and in the light of day from the essence of humanity. We call those people for whom the essence of humanity is animal and we call those human beings for whom the essence of humanity is divine. Similarly, we are people while we draw our essence from the realm of the animal or soul-like and we are human beings while we draw our essence from god.

By the same token do we differentiate between live humanity and the realm of the extinct. Myth as language facilitates the expression of ultimate reality. Whatever is live participates to an extent or wholly with its own nature in the nature of the good, which is goodness, since goodness is the nature of god, and god participates wholly in his own nature. Male and female springs from good, successively and successfully. Successively, in time, where one thing happens before the other and another happens afterwards, we give the name male to the first manifestation of the good and female to the second. Successfully, in space, where all things happen at the same time virtually, male and female coincide as simultaneous manifestations of the good, and we say that they come together for the sake of procreation.

In reality however there can be time without space but not space without time, just as there can be male without female but not female without male. Now this must be understood aright because it underlies as a basis the happiness of our existence on earth. The fact that there can be male without female in reality is a risk and a test, towards evil or good. In the same way the fact that there can be no space without time is a safety and a security, and the fact that there can be no female without male is a confidence and a consolation.

When we say that something is in reality, we imply that it is human because there can be no reality in extinction and humanity stops where extinction begins. But people, who espouse extinction, insist on calling all that reality which appeals to their senses alone and to nothing else, so that whatever appeals to their senses especially or specifically is immediately rejected and treated with contempt. Consequently it not only matter a great deal how a human being behaves towards people, but the issue is crucial. We have mentioned kindness. We do ourselves a disservice if we treat people unkindly. But the knowledge of what kindness amounts to, and equally of what it excludes, can only be gained in a relative conduct vis-à-vis people. Strictly speaking, human beings are not capable of kindness towards each other, where the love of brothers and sons, of sisters and daughters is of the essence and where a kindness must always suggest an oversight or a lack of consideration, but then we may readily forgive each other these kindnesses. On the other hand, many a human being whose kindnesses have not found a response becomes too embittered to love, and this is a pity.

And when we come across a popular element in ourselves or in each other, should we not then too practice a forgiving kindness? But love overrides in any case and cleanses of popularity.

And who are the people? Be careful you do not ask: Who are they really? and: What, in reality, are people? for people are not real and they cannot have any connection with reality. Therefore ask instead: Who and what are human beings? and employ your critical instinct in the service of that search, not judging but discriminating, between riches and varieties of human being. Then, where your love cannot harvest, be kind.

Myth as language allows us to deal with people in kindness so that nothing is lost and everything is brought home. Wherever extinction seems to hold sway, we trust that we may be kind. For people have said in their hearts that god is an idol and that humanity is at a loss. They have turned their senses finally towards one another in a celebration of popularity, where no human being shall interfere. It would be wrong for a human being to interfere where popularity has found itself.

So from the start one feels one ought to be tactful. One gets the impression that people are liable to do themselves harm, perhaps by overextending themselves, if one taxes too much their imagination or if one makes uncommon demands on their faculties in general.

But people in general, as the public, as we conceive of them now, have nothing to offer except a kind of resistance, an unwillingness in the face of humanity, and this unwillingness can never be expressed individually but it remains collective.

The collective unwillingness of people in the face of humanity must be trusted or it gets out of hand. One trusts that it will not get out of hand and such trust is effective. Suspicion or fear that it may get out of hand are simply signs of a lack of trust and of an increasing collective popular unwillingness, due to a certain lack of trust. Also, in an absence of trust, this collective unwillingness cannot be studied or analyzed or in any way understood but it simply gets out of hand.

Then external measures are required, to reverse the process, so that an unwillingness shall become an insistence, and while first we had an unwillingness to be human we now have an insistence on inhumanity, and again on account of a lack of trust. These two phases then can be identified, like flood and ebb of the tide, or like any other elemental cycle.

And these phases can be identified equally well in the case of individual people as of nations, and certain people behave like empires, others again like political states, which testifies to the elemental constitution of these alternating phases of collective unwillingness or insistence. The thing that undergoes these phases can be referred to as a unit, so that we have individual units and political units, alike in their appearance, of which a description is possible, though only while undertaken in trust and for the sake of trust.

All proper descriptions of these units, whether individual or political, result in more trust and in greater trust, and if we believe such a description, we will gain from it, but an improper description, in itself popular, in its effect captious or fractious, if believed, destroys belief, so we must be on our guard against improper description, and wherever we come across it, the thing to do is not to believe but to trust, since that is after all what is lacking.

The simple practical way of going about this is that we always at least trust, and then, as soon as we see an opportunity to believe we take it. If we have made a mistake, this will come home to us in the sense that our belief is destroyed or negated as soon as we undertake it, and there will also be detectable a sense in which our trust would change into gullibility, so that we right away feel like gulling our neighbours and spreading the spoof. The tendency to enthuse in public about popular works makes itself felt like that and if we give in to it or criticize its appearance we are fooled, in one way or the other.

*

Due to the fact that we are able to make use of myth as language, we may assure ourselves of an existential benefit from wherever we touch on the realm of the extinct, tactfully, trusting and in kindness, and in order to understand how this works we will first of all have to come to some conclusions with regard to what is generally called man's existence on earth, a time-honoured idea, and man's existence on earth in peace and happiness, an equally time-honoured ideal.

The first thing to be noted is that when we speak cheerfully about 'man's existence on earth' we find ourselves light-years away from your and my existence on earth. An idea intrigues us, an ideal draws us, but woe to him who attempts to transfer his idea to reality, who undertakes to translate his ideals into action. Ideas may well grow into ideals but then death has to claim them or else they draw him who holds them into extinction. God himself, we hear, was once an ideal, and then he died, otherwise today he could not be a reality.

But from this we know that live existence is all of a number of personal relationships. The father/son relationship of god in existence sets the pattern for it. We cannot know this relationship as an idea but only insofar as it makes a difference to our lives.

The father/son relationship of god in existence sets the pattern for all other relationships that all add up to our personal existence on earth. There is my relationship with myself, with my personal humanity, which makes me a son, and there is my relationship with you, or with your personal humanity, which makes me your friend and brother.

Then there is our relationship with our environment which makes us dwellers on the earth. This is the one we wish to examine more carefully now.

By environment here we mean everything that surrounds us, both within and without, that does not dominate or condition or in any way influence us, but we remain free in it and it remains free of us, regardless of interaction, communication and personal distinction.

This freedom is unique. Once we have tasted it we want to have it and we will give everything else up for it.

More specifically we call it the freedom to exist and it has to do with our life here on earth. The life we mean is not an idea but a whole reality. The only reason why we use the word existence rather than the word life is that we wish to specify that particular aspect of our life which has to do with our dwelling on the earth. So actually we should always call it relative existence, or our existence as relatives and as related, so as never to confuse it with individual, independent and impersonal existence, which cannot be free, and far from being an aspect of real life, it masquerades as a foundation for life which is delusory.

The father/son relationship of god, then, is the pattern, and the intrinsic pattern, of this relative existence, this existence where nothing can be found or done that is not related, and in just this peculiar way is it related that the father/son relationship of god is accessible there, as the pattern for any other relation.

This accessibility there will occupy us further. First we have to mention that it cannot be written about, but it can be written. It cannot be talked about but it can be spoken. It cannot be thought over but it can be thought.

The nub of our existence here is a combination of doing and being that cannot be separated, and if we exist here, rather than merely existing, we are and we do, so that being and doing are not forms of our existence but they are our existence. The only reason why we have a duality, albeit in connection, is that we have chosen for the time being to look at our existence on earth as an aspect of our life, and we want to limit ourselves, for the sake of science, to that aspect in itself, which can legitimately and profitably be done; as long as we then do not mistake the working duality in existence of doing and being for something that has meaning when we live.

So much in preparation.

The best example of existence here and now, in relative freedom, is our own personal commitment, in terms of life on earth, not to one thing or another, but as a person. Where I commit myself personally like this, I let myself be known as someone who can be relied upon for personal perfection.

The fact that personal perfection exists in terms of personal commitment and nowhere else, draws our attention to the existence such a state of affairs implies. When we commit ourselves to something, or if we seek perfection independently of a commitment, we may live for a time or we may look forward to life later, but we cannot exist here and now. In order to exist here and now, a certain consciousness is required of our internal dependence and of our external freedom, otherwise, in the absence of such consciousness, we must exist, either here or now, so that our existence is necessary or a duty.

A certain amount of attention paid by us specifically to that aspect of our life which we call life on earth reveals it as illuminating experience, and whatever use we make directly of such experience stands us in good stead and allows us to have an effect to the good where otherwise we would only be able to contribute in a hopeful manner. But an effect to the good, which is doubtless or infallible, and which may be described as investment of our personal perfection, is the highest form of life conceivable and the greatest life livable and beyond it cannot be gone, so there we exist fully as ourselves and the rest is satis-faction.

*

Myth as language places us in the unique position where we can rearrange all our concepts of life around us with impunity, and so, where a new order of those things is called for, there is no need to fight an old order or to compromise with it but we simply go ahead and let this new order speak for itself, in the presence of whatever just makes itself apparent.

Relative existence as we mean it, life on earth here and now as a personal commitment of our perfection, is in fact such a new order, and since it knows no barriers of sense or intellect, we may complacently call it the new order.

We bring about the establishment of this new order by way of kindness and trust wherever we come into contact with the realm of the extinct, and this is the existential benefit from there which we mentioned earlier. How we picture this depends entirely on our own singular person-ality. We must appreciate however that it cannot happen as a continuous state, but more like a series of interrup-tions of such a state, where the actual establishment in-strumentally goes on – not while we watch but when we do not watch. Then we may wait and know what goes on and understand what happens rather than tear our hair or rack our brains, mistaking the continuity of surface ap-pearances for something else; rather than break our hearts and attack our environment, in ignorance of the silent footsteps over invisible soil as our territory is marked out, when we have made new inroads.

The establishment of this new order, which we have elsewhere called the establishment of the kingdom of heaven on earth, or simply of the kingdom, signals its progress but not its progression. We can tell, in retrospect, that we have made progress, but we cannot tell that we are presently making it, not from signals or signs, that is, but we say that we take it on trust. Since no manipulation of environment is effected, we may take progress for granted.

This phenomenal activity which we have called watching, which may also be called observation, is not designed to add to our knowledge or to gain us any new insight but it must be seen to be conservative in nature, conservative, in fact, of existential establishment in progress. Perhaps the nature of it might be more explicitly termed if we describe it as a case of tending and wending. We know for a fact why we do it and what we have in mind while we do it but we do not have in mind a particular goal for it nor do we attempt to involve reason or appeal to reason. When we wrongly try to involve reason, we become convicted of stupidity and if we appeal to reason, mistakenly again, we stray into idiocy. The way out of such peripheral states of aberration is not by force or with violence but by means of restraint on the intellectual faculty, a kind of drawing back out of conflict and away from interference. The desire to break through, through a barrier that does not exist, of course, except due to an untimely appeal to reason, can become quite strong, and may be experienced as a kind of psychosomatic, episodic push or 'Schub' (in German), as a threat to a mental perspective or to a physical state of symmetry or harmony, and reactions to this again result in someone

174

going crazy or running amok, while fears and anxieties concerning the possibility or probability or likelihood of such reaction are called panic, neurosis and psychosis, in that order. The barrier itself therefore should be recognized as early as conceivable, not as a fatal device but as a fortuitous constraint, itself already in the interest of freedom, and trying to remove it or overcome it is akin to biting the hand that feeds us. Cleverly then we give in to it and smartly we abide by it, increasing only perhaps the degree of our endless and goalless watchfulness, in the interest of what we know to be the case, namely the insignificant and untested progress of our existential establishment.

All that pertains to this analogous state of endless watching and waiting, in comparison, on one hand (on the left), to the progress of the kingdom, which is our eternal dwelling on earth, and in relation, on the other hand (on the right), to life in general and in reality, which is our eternal gift or blessing, here and now and forever – all this tending and wending in nature, as we put it, in a conservative interest – we call world. And we do not call it the world, since the world has an end, or had an end, but the end of the world is world, which is world without end. Whether the world has an end or had an end, and whether the end of this world is world or was world, depends entirely on our own personal progress, and on whether we have arrived or hope to arrive; and this is not contradictory or in contention with any traditional view of things, since the world has always been recognized to be objective or subjective, while world can be neither but remains real, becomes real, in itself, not as a thing among things, or as the thing in itself, but named, judiciously: world in itself.

Now world as such, or world in itself, since it has no end, and since nothing can interfere with it or disturb it while nevertheless it is what it is in the light of day, affords us a most marvellous presence, so that we may be most wonderfully here now.

But naturally and spontaneously we wish to praise this and to admire the fact that it is so. World seems to uplift us into itself by eliciting this praise from us but at the same time we know that we ourselves are the agents of what goes on.

Others may be attracted by what we praise and good for them if they are but we do not praise so that others are attracted. We praise because we wish to do so. It fulfils us to overflowing and it is in itself an overflowing. And again, it is possible to know this perfectly and understand it wholly, to do it and be it, not in terms of reason, however, where divisions are made so as to discover the ground of things, nor on the basis of imagination either, when we create in order to complete creation – but mythologically, where we do what we are and we are what we do.

Our home, therefore, this eternal dwelling-place, comprises both the world we live in and the life we live, and the only reason we differentiate between the two is that we draw back and study, to gain knowledge, while we pretend for the time being that there could be such a thing as a difference between the world we live in and the life we lead, but we realize that the difference is ourselves, stepping back in wonder, even lost in admiration, but mostly at home in praise.

World is our home while we praise, and if we praise our home specifically, world is mythology.

*

World as mythology:

It gives me pleasure to be able to announce to all the world, and I have no compunction in stating.

A sentence such as this startles at first, and we take note of the fact that we are quite aware of how awkwardly it suits the contemporary sensibility.

But first it has to suit us, that much is clear. In a sense we are faced with the chance of praise praising itself, where anyone not in the know is bound haphazardly. We must make a contact however, not as a shortcoming but for orientation.

World grows from the tiniest seed and eventually our life is taken over by it. But world as knowledge is initially an expressive entity, where we bypass the concept-forming reason and the image-making faculty, whatever we want to call it, so that knowledge is more of a state of being for us: we are knowing – we are insofar as we know .

This knowledge, not of one thing or another but of itself, is best called reflection, and will not accommodate itself to a system or to any systematic and planned activity. What we previously called 'tending and wending', this expresses most perfectly to my own personal satisfaction at the moment what we do when we reflect like this, and when we cannot say upon what we reflect, but we simply reflect. I am a person after all, and a person

177

has no need of an opposite. This is what it means to be a person, that I can do without necessarily having to do something. This was implied and initiated in the very first sentence of this chapter.

So knowledge, when a person does it, called personal knowledge, is not at all the same as when an individual person does it, first of all, and certainly not the same as when people do it. This we must first of all get into our heads.

Personal knowledge, specifically described as reflection, puts me in contact with world. This is so because this knowledge is not only what I do but also and at the same time what I am. By knowing I am what I do and do what I am : this is a fortuitous shape and we should not be afraid of returning to it now and again, to refresh our memory.

By the same token, if we come to talk now not of knowledge done but of knowledge had, then we see how the knowledge I have is the knowledge we have. I have none of my own which you do not have, and you have none I do not have.

So we say that personal knowledge, where we have it, is communal. But to have knowledge, like anything else, means to possess it and to wield the power of it.

The way we have knowledge is by consciousness of the fact that we have knowledge. To the popular mind this amounts to yet one more contradiction 'in causa', and so it is meant to do, while a personal commitment cannot help but fluently comprehend, and immediately so.

Since a person is always committed (people are never committed) and individual persons only some of the time, there the power of personal knowledge is wielded and world is made plain. Consequently it reveals its establishment, its character as established. Making it plain is not like explaining, because the explained thing arises out of an unexplained thing, while world is made plain insofar as it is made.

Contact with world due to personal knowledge does not imply world independent of such contact or prior to it, just as world being made plain due to the power of personal knowledge does not imply world confused prior to the exercise of a power or independent from it.

Once we have contact with world and world made plain, also personal knowledge or reflection that we do and are, and then personal knowledge that we have, communally, we may go on from there with a cause and apply our knowledge, or put it to good use.

Remember that so far world is a contact and a consciousness. Also, it is not something we contact and are conscious of. The critical spirit, which stood by us when we dealt with the world, where contact automatically implied something contacted and where consciousness implied something of which one was conscious, stands behind us now, looking away from us, guarding our back, so that world may remain unworldly.

Because world bears no attributes. It cannot be described. The critical spirit sees to that, though inadvertently; behind us, as it were.

But world is like a cloud, and the wind blows it in from the sea until it covers all the land, so that no one can see it, yet we all draw benefit from its moisture.

And again, world is like many kind words spoken throughout a day, and if anyone were to ask who spoke them he would get no answer but the kindness does him good nevertheless.

So world is not attributable and it bears no attributes, but for the sake of those who prefer the world we may say what it is like. This is not a description of world, then, but a description of something else in terms of world. Because where we are and do and have knowledge, so that world is established for us, we offer that knowledge as a gift, which means we become fruitful and bear fruit.

World is not attributable and it bears no attributes: we become fruitful and bear fruit.

We offer our personal knowledge, which means we are fruitful, and we offer it in terms of world, which means we bear fruit.

Once world is established with us and we feel secure in our personal knowledge, being it, doing it and having it, we naturally wish to come out of ourselves and we look for ways of doing this, asking: How can we offer what we are and do and have, and to whom shall we offer it?

So there is one who knows this and he is the knowledge on offer. He is the one in whom all personal knowledge resides, yours and mine, which is the knowledge you do and are or the knowledge I do and am, and also ours, which is the knowledge we have.

He is the one on whose terms we offer our knowledge, and his terms are the terms of world. He is in fact the one in whom all world rests. And where we offer our knowledge, in terms of world, he returns on his own terms. Our offer or our personal knowledge and his return in person are one and the same. Considering what world is, and since it thrives on personal knowledge, it should not surprise us that world too is eventually personal, and that in the event of that person we say that he returns. Nevertheless this surprises. Always and again we are surprised by it, and what a surprise! But those who were established in their personal knowledge will find it a most pleasant surprise, while those who are not thus established will find themselves overshadowed or judged, so that then they too may establish themselves.

Mythology is knowledge for the sake of understanding myth, and at this point, when we have chosen to write world as mythology, remembering that we cannot write 'of' or 'about' world since world is devoid of attributes, it might pay us to draw attention to the fact that scientific knowledge, where pursued in a live way, like any other live science, and not in extinction, is knowledge for the sake of understanding something and not knowledge 'of' one thing or another. Live scientific knowledge is knowledge with a purpose and not of a thing. Its purpose defines it. And this purpose is understanding, or the understanding of something, as in our present case myth. But what kind of knowledge is it that is caused by understanding and the purpose of which is the understanding of something?

Only if we return to our senses and to the process of sensation can we answer that question, because each one of our senses, such as the sense of vision for example, may be turned outward, so as to take in appearances, or inward upon itself, reflectively. When we say that our sense of vision, say, is turned outward we do not mean outward from us but outward from itself, so that the mental pictures we harbour from time to time and the physical images we so often hold dear, while they cannot be said to exist outwardly with respect to another individual, they nevertheless do so for our sense of vision, and when this sense is exercised reflectively it has nothing to do with appearances, mental or physical, but only with our understanding, to which it contributes.

This should not mislead us now into supposing that there is an understanding independent or away from such sense contribution. There is hypocrisy, to which no sense contributes, and there is superstition, which successfully avoids sense, but neither of these has anything to do with understanding. As a matter of fact they oppose and negate it.

So knowledge is outward, of one thing or another, or inward, towards understanding.

The other thing to settle here is whether the outward and the inward sense of vision have anything other than their name in common. We do after all define knowledge of things in terms of those things while knowledge towards understanding has nothing of things in it or about it and so it cannot be defined but has to be described, and this to the extent that understanding succeeds and not at all in terms of that which is understood, if anything.

But in order to get on with this particular problem we would do well to keep before us the unforgettable notion of understanding as a total personal activity rather than as a process that may go on one sense at a time, like knowledge. True enough, the whole person may know, but this is in a category of its own, which we might call intuitive contemplation, or something like that, so rarely does it occur, but in the case of understanding it comes to pass that the whole person must understand or else there is no understanding at all.

This much being agreed, we need only to add that the difference between understanding, such as when you or I understand, period, and the understanding of something, such as when I understand myth, is whether knowledge is contributed for a purpose or for a cause. Understanding itself cannot be a cause, but can be the purpose of vision, of inward, contributory vision, while the understanding of myth, or of any other thing, can be a cause, in which case knowledge is contributed effectively.

So the cause of our knowledge presently is the understanding of myth and all our available senses contribute to that cause.

While we gain scientific knowledge, we do not become blind to external things of course. Or do we? During the course of scientific knowledge we certainly remain aware of everything because we continue to exist in the light of day. But it would be difficult to say how anything is external. As we become accustomed to world, it occurs to us that the distinction of internal from external, as in the case of internal vision or vision towards understanding rather than towards a house or a car, was instigated for the sole purpose of returning our vision to its rightful order, and since we discovered it involved and embroiled in such a way that things had become external, we called upon it to turn and chose to call that internal, but still in terms of something other than our understanding, namely external things, just as previously we had called them our external senses in terms of external things. We can see therefore that the external-internal distinction was an instrumental one and that it can be laid down as soon as the operation is complete.

It is true therefore that we do not become blind to the house and to the car, but they are not any more external to our sense of vision. Nor, of course, are they internal to it, as we just showed. We cited them as examples of things that do not at a certain time contribute to our understanding. Then we said that during knowledge we nevertheless remain aware of them.

And this is where their attributes come in.

We remain aware, or are aware, of those things which do not at a certain time contribute to our understanding and in this awareness, or as part of it, they attribute to our understanding, even though we have no knowledge of them as such and consequently do not understand them.

Our understanding, to which all our knowing contributes, is the main business, like the inside of the cup, while our awareness of everything else is also important, like the outside of the cup.

In the same way our main business as human beings is that we love one another, and then it is also important that we are kind to people.

*

World as mythology reveals its innermost secrets, and this is in fact the use of mythology, that it leads us, gently and persuasively, to the heart of that realm where everything that is wanted may be gained merely by asking for it. Also it teaches us how to ask, so that we do not waste time and energy asking for wind when we want power and asking for flame when we want warmth or heat. Far too many of us have made up our minds as to the means to happiness and we ask for those means instead of asking for happiness. So it matters a great deal how we prepare ourselves for the times ahead.

Knowledge, we have decided, is not of external matters, but these become part of our awareness as attributes to our understanding. We have no business meddling with our awareness of things and we should never try to analyze what lies 'out there' as though it could be taken to pieces or altered to suit us, because what must suit us is derived from our knowledge and if anything lies 'out there' we have sufficient cause for an increase in knowledge. If instead we interpret this accidental externality as though it were reality we soon go astray and surround ourselves with a tissue of lies.

Knowledge is not of external things, nor of internal things or entities for that matter, but of myth and of world and of reality. These three are one. And if we truly have knowledge of something rather than knowledge towards the understanding of something, that is to say knowledge in itself rather than knowledge with a purpose or for a cause, then we have knowledge of myth, of world or of reality. The one that concerns us here is knowledge of myth.

*

Knowledge of myth:

We have mentioned how it occurs now and again that things appear as outside of our senses, or external to them, and that this is our signal, not for trying to know them and for accumulating extinct knowledge, which is useless and becomes a burden to us, but for scientific knowledge, which is knowledge for the purpose of understanding or for the sake of understanding something, and then those 'external' things work as awareness-attributes towards our understanding. Scientific knowledge is not extinct but live, and knowledge of things that are not external, nor internal for that matter, but spiritual, is live too and, as we indicated at the end of the previous chapter, spiritual knowledge is of myth, of world or of reality, so that these three are one, all knowledge of the spirit, or knowledge of all beings, and not of things which are but figments of our imagination, delusions of our brain or tricks of our heart.

In practice what counts of course is that we gradually wean ourselves away from extinct or non-knowledge and that we learn how to cope with our faculties when time and again they become constricted and extracted from us in such a way that our loss increases instead of our knowledge.

The mistakes we make about extinct life and its collection of dead things cannot be at one and the same time

recognized as mistakes and applied by way of rectifica-
tion.

In the past, various systems of knowledge and doctrine
were set for us, as turning points, to help us turn away
from carnal extinction and towards an ideal or a state of
hope, and as way stations, where we might rest for a
while and arrive at a sober point of view and develop a
sensible perspective. Schools of thought urged us in the
right direction, literature and the arts consoled us in our
pain, cleansed and refreshed us.

Religion was organized in this way and that way, as
public worship and as private devotion, so that our conduct in the open might be geared towards less detrimental
goals and so that in our individual behaviour we could
look to allegories for encouragement and to symbols for
comfort. The various ritual beliefs of these Religions as
they were called to signify their extinction could operate
for us as authoritative disciplines if we chose.

But the accent, in all of this help that was offered, was
always on a free choice according to our best lights at the
time, and where help was not offered but constraint imposed, pressure applied and obligation laid on, as though
one could make a new man or punish his way to freedom,
there we came face to face once again with extinction,
only this time perhaps in the guise of our alleged best interests, domination dressed up as parental care.

Then as now, however it came our way, our choice lay
in the avoidance of extinction and in the harvest of life.
East or west, in intellect or desire, the aim was the same:
north or south, in doing or being, there was one pursuit.
The elements return to the earth, souls go to heaven. The

spirit that is god becomes man and enters into human beings, so that if they accept that spirit they may become human beings and not die, rushing away from life deeper into extinction.

As we turn our attention more specifically now to knowledge of myth, and of things insofar as we regard them as myth or they present themselves to us as myth, we may perhaps do well to keep in mind that we are not dealing with a category of knowledge or in a form of it, since categories and forms pertain to at least some aspect of an abstracting activity, such as when we mean to distinguish real from spurious knowledge and helpful from wishful thinking; but we are dealing with good spirit itself, listening to it and conversing with it, and the outcome of this is knowledge as myth. Or again, we know that spirit and it becomes myth for us, myth entirely, not myth as a partial emanation of the whole spirit nor myth as a finite revelation of the infinite spirit, all of which still clings to various more or less helpful thought categories, but myth as the spirit.

If first we seek the kingdom of heaven, we may now go ahead and be the kingdom, which is the kingdom of heaven on earth. Why now and not in the past? Only because of the advent of the spirit as myth. To know this means to be able to take advantage of it.

We know it especially with our hearts. Therefore we call it heartfelt knowledge. It originates there as a genitive inscription of the law and is also consummated there, as the ultimate perfection of that law in deed.

But when we speak of the law of the spirit today we do not immediately hold an audience. The spirit today avoids audiences and makes itself felt as myth, not on formal occasions, prepared for the event, but when we least expect it.

So the law of the spirit today might be described as a series of unexpected events, as long as we keep in mind that any such series cannot bear any resemblance to any other one. If it did we would again be dealing with a formula or with a repetition of matter, which betoken not the spirit today but a spirit of the past or of the present .

The law of the spirit today is heartfelt knowledge of myth, and in our heart we may recognize the various lineaments of this knowledge, especially if we take into account that we are the kingdom, and that therefore in our hearts we share in a single interest, which is the being of the kingdom.

Not one person is the kingdom but at least two or three who decide together that their being should amount to knowledge of myth, so as to this much they are in agreement and know themselves of a single body and mind. This knowledge manifests itself in the way they behave towards one another, in the care they take and in the consideration they deem worthwhile, but most of all they recognize one another as members of a single family, the family of man. But the family of man is no sentimental idiom, no idealist notion of peace on earth, but my concrete relation to you as my brother or sister. I do not treat you as though you were my brother or sister, but I know you to be that and I relate to you as such. My relation to you, insofar as I instigate and maintain it, will be that determined by the fact that we have the same father and mother. By our father I mean him who gives us being and by our mother I mean her who supports us in that being.

We call him who gives us being father. That our being is given to us and not taken by us or accidental to us should go without saying, but sometimes we forget, and then our being is withdrawn from us, and this draws to our attention that we have no power over the origin of our being. So we can decide <u>what</u> we are but not <u>that</u> we are. And if we decide to be a person, for example, rather than just an individual, we obviously take it for granted that being itself should be available to us and that personality, which is the being of a person, should be accessible to us.

Once we have decided that our being should be the good, or god, rather than the bad, we soon discover, by trial and error if not by instruction and insight, that good being becomes available to us as a relation and that it becomes completely available to us, to the fullness and overflowing of our nature, as a familiar relation.

The essence of a relation is that we turn back to something once we have discovered that we can turn away from it.

That the good should be available to us in relation rather than as a natural evolutionary process or progression makes immediate sense when we acquaint ourselves with our sense of perfection and with our desire for complete satisfaction and for utter fulfilment, for these, showing how we are made, as sovereign in our humanity, contain, upon inspection and examination, a gift or talent of good, laid up there for us, as an inheritance, to be claimed.

If and when we turn to the good, in a relation, our very being becomes good and soon we can see no difference between what we desire, what we sense as perfection, and what becomes available to us. If we did busy ourselves with such a difference, our inheritance would not be claimed but squandered or neglected.

So whenever we come to any obstruction to our desire for perfection in goodness, we may take it as encouragement to turn and relate to the good, and the good can have nothing to do with this obstruction, not in sense nor in intellect, so turning away from the obstruction does not get us closer to the good because we would still take our orientation from that obstruction.

Surrounded by hindrances, barriers and obstructions, but fired by a sense of perfection, a thirst for justice, steeped in a desire for it, how can we turn to the good and where do we find it? Whatever attempts we make to remove those hindrances only alter their appearance and aggravate our state.

We said that the essence of a relation is that we turn back to something once we have discovered that we can turn away from it. Now we can add that the essence of a personal relation is that we do turn back to a person once we have discovered that we can turn away from him or her.

Since we desire to be persons and since there can be no difference between us and the good once we have decided to turn to it, it stands to reason that if I am a person so must personhood be an attribute of god, else how could I even desire to be a person.

When I as a person turn towards god as a person, having realized that I can move away, this is a familiar relation, and since good being flows from this relation, being the issue of it, the person to person relationship between me and god, between myself and the good, must be a son and father relationship, because that is the name we customarily give to the relation between two persons where one depends on the other for being.

It remains only to ask: How is it possible for me to turn to god as a person? I realize that I am able to do it and I can observe myself doing it, quite irrespective of all hindrances, barriers and obstructions, but I certainly could not explain to anyone else how to go about it and in that respect I seem to be completely ignorant.

Since I cannot explain, by signs and such, how I do it but find myself doing it nevertheless, and indeed find myself wanting to do it, I can only suppose that it has been done and that I follow. Someone somewhere along the line must have cut a path through this jungle because, as you can see, I am able to make my way through it.

So if I am a son, returning to my father, precisely a son because I return to him, there must have been another son, the very first one, in whose footsteps you and I follow. Curiosity inclines us to ask who he was but more than that, gratitude fills us for the fact that he was.

And, given that he was, considering what he must have been since no obstruction, barrier or hindrance has stopped him or even slowed him down, he must still be, else something would have put a stop to him. So since he still is, it must be possible for us to get to know him, in the flesh, right here and now, and we discover that this is in fact the case. Not insofar as we freely return in person to our father as sons and daughters is this the case, but rather insofar as we recognize each other doing so and as we wish one another well.

*

Mutual recognition and welcome of all of god's sons and daughters, including the first, the one who came first and made life for the rest of us possible; and our wise dependence as children on our father, our prudent acceptance of our mother's guidance: all this is what we mean by the knowledge of myth. First we must know that god is our father and when we acknowledge him as such, not as someone who adopts us but as someone whose very being, which is goodness itself, works miracles in our hearts and operates in our souls, then we can bring up children of our own and be exemplary fathers to them, teaching them early who their real father is and in what way they are our real brothers and sisters, for an effective father brings up his children as god's children, and learns his fatherhood from our real father, while our children learn best from us insofar as we are god's children, not insofar as we insist that we are their real fathers, who pay lip service to an idealized version of morality. Also we as parents can learn from our children the wisdom of childhood, which makes us truer children of god.

Now if a father is one on whom we can depend for our being, then she is a mother who consoles us and brings us together under one roof.

Consolation is ours when we grow in the spirit and our organic requirements change so that a relative darkness descends and we experience terror, horror or grief. So that these three do not overcome us and we do not succumb to them, our mother, who is one with our father out of a specific distinction, mitigates our experience and makes it bearable. Not that we first have to ask our mother but she gives unsolicited, and therein resides our consolation.

If we recognize her as our mother, we not only have consolation for ourselves but we may pass that consolation on to one another, so that we have it in community. Living in community in fact implies a mutual consciousness and exchange of this personally ready consolation.

As for bringing us together under one roof, this has to do with our manifold urges for domesticity and with our instinct for sharing in a single outlook on life.

An outlook on life is what we have when we value a settled existence and eschew the production of upheavals for their own sake.

Here it should perhaps be mentioned that we cannot know our mother, by way of recognition and consciousness, until we have at least a notion of the kingdom, which is the kingdom of heaven on earth, and that we cannot feel and build on the security after which we hanker until we have gained a sound foundation in the reality of our father as made known and comprehensible to us by his firstborn son. We may say therefore that when we hanker for security and feel proverbially like a motherless child we should turn to our father who then gives us our mother.

Specifically now, an outlook on life and a feeling of security are maternal benefits in the true sense of the word. An outlook on life may be fostered and a feeling of security may be cherished.

But the first benefit of a proper outlook on life as a description of domesticity is a liberal concept of mankind, to go along with our free perception of humanity. A liberal concept of mankind allows us to acknowledge, on a common basis of compassionate disinterest and in a spirit of impartial sympathy, the Jew and the Christian, the Chinese and the Russian, the Communist and the Capitalist, and makes it possible for us to handle the strange fires of creed, ethic and idiom.

We call it a proper outlook on life because it does not infringe against creed, ethic and idiom and suchlike but helps us give due weight and value to committed elements; we avoid cynicism, sarcasm and criticism, but not at the expense of a sense of proportion and perspective. In the same way does a liberal concept of mankind help us stay clear of all judgement in general or in particular. Sympathy and compassion as emotion states; impartiality and disinterest as mind dynamics: along these lines we are given support so that we may remain secure while our world is changed.

A settled existence does after all imply a changing world. We may feel urges for domestic life, in the way that this is meant here, but there is nothing we can do to bring it about, since it comes about when the time is ripe. A false domesticity is usually brought about when we try to stop our world from changing, whereas genuine domesticity comes along when we have what it takes to abide with our world as it changes, and this necessary increment is an image of world.

We said that if we recognize her as our mother we not only have consolation but we have it in community, which is a real boon. If we also acknowledge her as our mother she not only brings us together under one roof but she assigns to us specific duties there, through which we will be able to express our final need.

Such duties, which are not based on virtue or moral principle but undertaken by us spontaneously or on the spur of the moment, strange as that may seem, are sources of a most peculiar pleasure and elements of a singular joy. No one can hold us to them, and so our domesticity becomes vibrant, which is a blessing.

But even this business of being brought together under one roof might not be so easy to grasp. We have an idea of it perhaps, and we might picture it as everyone embraced by a single existential idea, but then we would have to ask: What about the idea itself? Is there such a thing as the idea? If so, what would it be and how could one approach it, think it or feel it? Could it be experienced?

Let us assume that the idea exists. We would not be able to ask, felicitously: Where does it come from? as we can in the case of ideas, because nothing could distinguish us from this idea in a way that would allow for a critical distance. But we have become so accustomed to this critical distance between our ideas and ourselves that we would judge it as foolishness if someone asked us to do without it. On account of it, after all, we may compare ideas, estimate their relative merit, evaluate each in its turn, and doesn't the way we do this distinguish us in our own eyes and in the eyes of our public and peers?

One idea at a time and at the expense of all others makes for fanaticism, we know that. Here however we assume that there is such a thing as the idea itself; not one among many, fanatically lifted to a false position, but in that position and of that stature right from the start.

What start?

Well, there must be an origin of ideas, one supposes, and since we are not allowed to ask where, perhaps we may ask: How? How does it come that ideas at one time occur and not at another time? Perhaps he who knows the time knows this too? And surely if he knows the time he will also know the idea?

Now we cannot know the time, no matter how many playful questions we ask, that goes without saying, but we know that there is such a thing as the time, and this is important.

When the time has come there is no getting around it. Too soon or too late may end in tragedy.

Not that ideas have a will of their own, no, we are not about to suggest that. But we do believe in this playful drive, and in its capacity for revealing the hitherto unrevealed. Because we believe in it, that is why it does it. And so it depends on timing and tact. Elsewhere these have been praised; we mean to extol them.

Timing reveals the time, tact the idea.

This is a shape. We have had several shapes recently: a liberal concept of mankind, that was one. Then there was a single outlook on life. And togetherness under one roof. And consolation in community. Then there was a notion of the kingdom and an image of world. All these are shapes. Not shapes of things to come, but final and unshakeable shapes, of a soundness and a subtlety that cannot be surpassed by definition.

Tact interests us especially at the moment because it reveals the idea. The idea plays into it. Not contact is what counts but tact. Contact implies impact, separation of duality, object and subject, this and that. Tact implies nothing else, only itself. In fact we might call it the implication extraordinaire. What we tactfully imply has a face of its own. It has visual completeness.

And tact makes headway with what we called the idea. We can remain 'in tact' without wondering what it is, or with what, but when we begin to wonder, as in a sense of play, then the idea is revealed. Not some particular idea, but the idea itself. Goethe suggested to Schiller that he experienced it, and indeed his personal tact made out Goethe's greatness precisely because of the smallness such tact requires of us. We must be incomparably small.

Only then can the idea find us out.

When it does so, we stand revealed to ourselves.

Oh that we should be minutely small when this happens. There are those who rush tactlessly out into the realm of the idea and they return bedraggled, limping, with their wings clipped.

Tact reveals the idea and only in revelation can the idea remain intact for us, for it will not be fragmented.

Nature, on the whole, is merely another word for the idea. Only here, instead of tact, we use proof.

We mentioned earlier how our mother may be recognized and acknowledged. Tact reveals the idea during this same process of recognition, and nature is proved while the acknowledgement goes on. See how one is the same as the other in this case: the recognition and the acknowledgement, the revelation and the proof.

Nature, not the nature of this or that but nature itself, is proved insofar as we systematically endure all its effects and thoroughly account for all of its causes.

But the endurance of natural effects involves organic stimuli, just as an account of natural causes explains carnal responses, and we do well to keep ourselves in mind of that.

Now both in the case of the revealed idea and on the occasion of proved nature are we 'brought together under one roof' and it serves us well indeed if we use our wits now and acknowledge our mother in this, so that 'our final need will find expression'.

We acknowledge our mother by confirming the assumption that she exists through the use of a name, and that name is Mary. Not that she existed is what we confirm, but that she exists now. The effects of nature we endure in her name and the causes of nature we account for in her name lead to the peace of mankind.

The peace of mankind is our final need, and it finds expression in what we do when we acknowledge our mother, confirming her existence now, by proving nature and revealing the idea in her name, which is Mary. If she had not existed we could not give her that name, for that was her name while she existed, and before she existed she had no name, though many acknowledged her. But now she exists and we call her Mary.

Knowledge of myth includes the recognition and acknowledgement of Mary, and those who call her by name have the added protection of a subtle body and of its emergence in the light of day. We mentioned earlier how the endurance of natural effects involves carnal stimuli and how an account of natural causes explains carnal responses. We should not try to think this through, but simply apply it, since evidence takes some time to accumulate. Not until tomorrow perhaps will we recognize the fruits of what we sowed today. So it is best to go on from hour to hour, perhaps in an epic vein, unwilling to develop a taste for glory but simply and modestly taking glory in stride. And if our vision should clarify world for us, due to our protection our senses are not enthralled, our flesh not captivated or charmed but quickened, our sense made shapely.

The perfection proper to Mary is shape. Even the shape of every human being is maternally inspired. We celebrate the inner stillness in the movement of shape. We carry ourselves with ease, abandoned to this shape that is ours. Not that we acknowledge Mary as our mother, but that we assume that our mother exists, and then we confirm this assumption by giving her the name she once had, this is how we account for it that even in this last day, which is also the first day, we become cognizant of the shape of things to be. We carry ourselves with ease in the knowledge of our inner perfection and what we outwardly show liberates and sets free.

*

Mother, you take us to task, for our
wildness, our inner unwillingness to be led.
Even our past shyness, where an
untrained brain kept love at arm's length,
leads us astray now, leaves us
precious little room for coping.

We collect stray thoughts, perfectly
at ease with ourselves for the duration of
a moment perhaps, while a fly settles
on our skin to make matters worse, or a
cold eye casts its shadow
where the heart has left an opening.

Here we have an example of tact revealing the idea,
during the process of our recognition of our mother, followed, or succeeded, by self-revelation. Words are, of
course, only one of an infinite number of means by which
such recognition can be exemplified. We go on now to
give a similar example, of her acknowledgment, and of
nature proved:

Small insect swirls the lamplight round,
on shadowed wall finds common ground,
shares equal worth with wood-pulp grain
on paper where these words refrain

from entering where a dull world roosts
and casts in dreams of flame and gold
all aspects of our love and lust
shielded by shroud of cosmic dust.

In Mary we take fledgling care
of me and you, while everywhere
a sphinx lies waiting, as in trance

to spark a death off, quite by chance.

The spirit today is myth and myth is the spirit, let us repeat that. Today is not a day that will one day be yesterday, but today is the day in which we live now, and we are live today, not extinct.

Knowledge of the fact that the spirit today is myth and that myth is the spirit we called heartfelt knowledge and such knowledge is in itself of a special benefit to us. Various implications may be ascertained.

If the spirit were not myth, it would have to be approximately deduced, which is to say: practically guessed at and sympathetically illustrated, always at the expense of some critical spirit, and therefore fragmented or as a system.

And this is in fact what happened, that critical spirit ran its course during the modern age, while the spirit was not yet myth, and it relied upon our willingness to be tempted and tested to further itself.

With the advent of myth as the spirit today, the critical spirit has become a thing of the past and we can say with confidence that we have that thing behind us, though it matters to some extent to whom we say it.

That the spirit is myth is the same as that the family of man is complete. All the family relations are at once spiritual and mythic. Fatherhood and motherhood, brotherhood and childhood, are all equally susceptible to concrete reality, and beyond this, as peace of mankind, we have the boon of friendship.

To know these relations as at once spiritual and mythic is to realize their fullest potential, and to understand this in turn is what we mean by church. Church, therefore, is the understanding of mankind as related in family and friendship. World, as world without end if we compare it to the world, to this world or that world, and church, as church without cause if we compare it to the church, to this church or that church: these are shapes, or shapes of things to be, if we compare them to shapes of things to come.

Church has no cause, but it is all effect. And considering its definition as understanding, and as the understanding, in particular, of mankind as related in family and friendship, we can see that it has no meaning and makes no sense outside of ourselves, although the understanding we mean, as of mankind, by ourselves, can never be an understanding by myself or yourself exclusively. My thinking of church therefore automatically includes or involves some of your thinking of church, and our feeling on it, as a matter of tact and timing, cannot be individualized.

Church thought and church feeling, which stem from the understanding of mankind as related in family and friendship, can therefore never be exclusive, or inclusive, for that matter, but if we were to describe it we would call it mutual. No individual can understand mankind as related, and from within our individuality we haven't a hope of even an inkling of what is meant by the family of man. From within our personality on the other hand we always strive towards community in any case, so this is where mutual thought and feeling must generally start and does in fact start in the particular, but again only insofar as it stems from familiar and kindly understanding, in humanity and friendship extended towards all mankind.

Church is all effect, which means that it operates as a key.

Introductory to the kingdom are those effects which stimulate the nerve system, namely neural effects, and these stem from our understanding insofar as we dwell in the light of day at some particular time. Not that we somehow produce these effects and introduce others to the kingdom, but rather that our mutual understanding, as described above, introduces us and others to the kingdom in the way that it relates, the kingdom consisting in relation.

Neural effects are felt and then fastened and finished. Feeling identifies them so that we are not carried away or stricken in some way, as would happen if we lacked the discipline which no one however can lack who is capable of mutual understanding; this particular insight aids us in our progress in reflection on any present individuality, where it explains certain reactions both typical and strange that otherwise have nothing else to do with us. Once identified however, these neural effects are fastened, or made fast, insofar as we refer them to our brain, and they are finished, or made finite, inasmuch as this reference is after all not to 'the' brain but to our brain, not to an ideal entity or a universal thing but to the particular brain we have and work with, so that instead of the neural effect becoming a neutral effect it remains charged, electrically, and rests as brain substance. Brain substance is a reference of electrically charged neural effects at rest.

In this particular instance then church facilitates the realization of an ideal, the ideal being the nerve system. The extent to which this ideal has been built up and constructed over the years and centuries must be obvious to even the casual student of comparative histories. Sex-related virtues especially fall into this category, along with sublimations of erotic desires, satisfaction of physical desires by way of utopia, culture as heightened tension and as intensification of class distinction, both in the mind and in the flesh; then all the various goals of education concurrent with an image or a concept of man, the intellectual patterns of society, political state, empire, to be achieved as far as possible, under strain, with comparative survival as the reward; the recipes, methods and disciplines for the salvation of other souls, the techniques for transporting someone from savage to sage, from sinner to saint: all the stress and strain and straits, to 'lift up the Son of Man', to fine-tune the nerves, your and my nerves, to a pitch where they would allegedly support themselves and one another in an ecstatic celebration of the effort that went into it, but secretly for the sake of the most perfect possible readiness, an optimal preparedness for something only dimly foreseen, only according to the shadow it played across the far side of the retina from beyond – but nonetheless: out of this world!

The nerve system was the ideal, though it wasn't often called that. The realization of this ideal through church, in particular through neural effects, we documented just now. The realization itself was spoken of as introduction to the kingdom, and as brain substance, available in reference. A reference to brain in the future, by ourselves to our brain, will be tantamount to an affirmation of the kingdom, which we are, and so an affirmation of ourselves.

Now in addition to the church effects that stimulate the nerve system we have those which aggravate the flesh. This sounds frightening at first, but not to worry. The work has already been done.

Once again we may notice that the flesh, like the brain in the previous section, is an ideal, and that the effects of church are to operate in the direction of the ideal's realization.

The way this ideal was fashioned in the past was mainly through organization, and through the organization of non-productive matter. One was of the impression that something was being built and one appreciated the process of construction, but that which carried the weight of the raw material and bore the burden of the inert matter was always the flesh, organized as highly as possible in order to render that weight negligible and to make that burden light. We can understand this quite clearly today because we have been brought face to face with it since our time has come around, but in those days we imagined and speculated and guessed and strove to do our best, after the manner of a performance, and it was all the same whether we constituted a state, constructed a cathedral, formed a symphony or designed a man, with his various humours or astrological tendencies, his blood circulation and musculature and skeletal make-up, his chemical balance and his electromagnetic sympathies, the machinery of his psyche, the fight and flight of his ghost: what counted was that after thinking of it as in parts, which we couldn't help, we then felt constrained or moved to fit those parts together in the way that most suited us, as we imagined, but principally to lessen the burden and diminish the weight of all flesh, of all partial and fragmentary and atomized matter. Wherever we looked we saw pieces, all flesh, and the idea was to make something out of those pieces, the flesh, which was the ideal, formed or constructed or manufactured, conjured magically or made up, and our reason for this was always fundamental and basic. We needed ground to stand on, a purpose for existing. Not to construct meant to be destroyed, to be atomized, to come to naught, which was, after all, 'the way of all flesh'.

But the flesh as such of course, as the ideal, was useless, just as a ladder in itself is useless, if we have nowhere to climb. A few realized what the ladder was for and they used it, but the great majority contented itself with building ladders. This is hardly anything worth despairing over today; I only mention it for the sake of context. In summation, between the experience of 'all flesh', of 'all is vanity', 'le néant' and the flesh as the highly organized, and these days super-sophisticated, ideal, stand all the so-called 'works of man, man as such of course being an ideal construct itself.

These 'works of man', or 'the temple' as it has been called, this brick by brick assembly of traditional ways and cultural artifacts, is aggravated by church, we have observed, and some of the effects that we mean by church are in fact an aggravation of this ideal.

But an ideal of which one tries to make use is an idol. To the extent that we try to make use of an ideal we commit idolatry and go from bad to worse.

Penal effects, on the other hand, as an aggravation of the flesh and as a realization of the ideal which we call the flesh, disturb us in our idolatry and harass us in our turpitude due to such idolatry, to such a falsification of a created purpose. Such disturbances and such harassment naturally cause us anxiety, and this anxiety is usually the first we know of the potentially beneficial penal effects, beneficial in terms of purification, purgation and general perfection.

Now where neural effects stemmed from our understanding of mankind as related in family and friendship insofar as we dwell in the light of day at some particular time, penal effects stem from that same understanding, but to the extent that we inhabit our proper and suitable existential sphere. Penal effects need not even come to our attention and may entirely underlie a set of circumstances completely at our disposal. When we have the anxiety we mentioned, we know that penal effects are potential and that therefore some adjustment is still to be made before a realization can occur. Such an adjustment is made most successfully in submission to that anxiety, while a reaction to it, instead of aggravating the flesh, aggravates our perilous situation. Submission to the anxiety, not to any spurious or supposed cause of the anxiety by the way, assures then that penal effects do not become perilous but that they come home to us, where the heart is, there to produce a change of heart most emphatically and at the very source. They come home to us insofar as they remain changed, rather than reverting to our peril, becoming peril; and where neural effects remained electrically charged and in a process of transformation towards rest, penal effects remain chemically changed and in a process of transmutation towards cover.

The meanings of rest and cover in terms of life in the light of day should be plain enough not to need elucidation.

Church is all effect, we have said, and when we view all effect as effects we are able to distinguish between neural effects and penal effects, and to these we now add final effects.

Final effects remain physically shaped and in a process of transubstantiation towards ground.

We found out earlier that electrically charged neural effects at rest are brain substance to which we refer, and that there is such a thing as heart substance, when chemically changed penal effects are forwarded to our heart and there we have cover. Our heart prefers them and we have them in preference to our heart, as cover. But final effects we defer to our body and we have ground in deference to our body; this comes as the third substance and we call it body substance.

None of these substances are due to church, since church is no cause, but they are church, all effect, not viewed as effects now but in use as substance.

Church in use is a highly recommended faculty of our human being, and it lends itself to a study most profitably under the auspices of our divine nature. We remember for the moment that divine nature and human nature are one, seen here in reference to god and there in comparison to its various manifestations as human being, and that this should not be confused with popular nature and supernature, because these two are never one but always and everywhere in separation.

So under the auspices of our divine nature we may study church in use, as brain substance, heart substance and body substance, and with this in the offing we may return for the time being to body substance in particular, because here too an ideal is being realized, not the flesh that is aggravated, as in the case of penal effects, nor the nerve system that is stimulated, as in the case of neural effects, but the body of knowledge that is remembered.

By the body of knowledge, rather than our body of knowledge, we mean the accumulation of derived material facts and figures, of imposed rules and regulations, of hypothetical explanations and justifications that man has come up with in the past to idealize his human condition, rendering it more bearable and less strange. All the temporal and temporary benefits of this endeavour should not be underestimated because they shorten the time and gain us many a respite, but they can be overestimated, if that body of knowledge is mistaken for our body of knowledge, for the one we have just recently identified in terms of church substance and as body substance. As a matter of fact where the ideal is mistaken for reality we actually forfeit the temporal benefits that should be ours, and where the idealization of man's condition is mistaken by him for a realization of himself, he loses the temporary benefits that might be his. The knowledge that encourages me to feel proud rather than dejected for being a British citizen, that allows me to cross the Atlantic by air in an hour so as to be able to undergo a sophisticated operation on my right eye: this is ideal knowledge, and where it is taken for real knowledge it leads to extinction; and of course where it is presented as though it were the real thing, it must be said to be extinct. It makes little difference whether the condition that is idealized is mental, carnal or physical, moral, ethical or political – what counts for our present purpose is that we recognize how such ideas are formed initially and always again out of a need for time and not as a basis of freedom, and how they arise on the basis of constraint and not out of a will for freedom.

So the sum-total of all ideas and of all the notions we attach to them and abstract from them, we can call the body of knowledge, and it stands in no real relation to us until we at least recognize that this is so, that in fact it does not stand in any real relation to us, and only then can we say, perhaps with Socrates, that we do possess a bit of wisdom insofar as we confess our ignorance with respect to ideal knowledge, or insofar as we know that ideal knowledge is not real and therefore not ours, and if we mean to have any real knowledge we must at least remember that ideas are not real, though hopefully we will progress from there, so that we will not stop worshipping in special buildings and on certain high places without right away worshipping in reality.

Memory and remembrance of individual pieces of ideal knowledge however is of no use, and if we wish to gain ground, we must remember ideal knowledge in toto, as the body of knowledge. The memory we mean involves critique, and as we work out a stance vis-à-vis ideal knowledge, we also develop the memory that is required to facilitate the process of transubstantiation towards ground.

So we might begin by allocating to our memory the task of vindicating our past and the past in general insofar as the two are connected. Such a vindication would first of all distinguish between what we know because we have allowed ourselves to be influenced and what we know because we have been accidentally impressed, and then it would gain us an insight into our immediate surroundings during that time as either imposed or liberal. It may come as a terrific shock to a person to discover how much of that past knowledge holds no water, and in order to be able to sustain that shock, one must be able to fall back on at least an increment of trust in the inviolability of one's human nature.

Critical memory, or memory in crisis, (not a criticizing memory or a memory in crisis) rejects ideas, even ideas of itself, not because we have anything against ideas but because all of our faculties seek to make contact, in such a case of memory, with their own source and origin, with the hold they have over themselves and on themselves as it were, so that we are dealing here with a very primary discipline and with a rather radical need for correspondence, that will not make do, for once, with slight of hand, currying favour with a public, or with conjuring tricks to entertain an audience. Ideas are rejected in the same way and for the same reason as a public is avoided and an audience prevented, so that we might for once remember on grounds of logic rather than derived and contrived, with aids and according to marks, in the direction of the past rather than around some aspect of the past.

But memory on grounds of logic leaves us singularly unsatisfied unless we curtail our various pleasure-drives and pain-repulsions and insist on a neat dislocation of truths from contexts of delusion – easier said than done: unless we insist on conceptual memory itself, so that we are memory rather than doing it, and sustaining ourselves there, as memory, maintaining our hold on our faculties with our faculties.

Ideally we would call this pure memory, as an approximation to what we mean but in reality we say what we mean completely and call it memory there.

Memory there has nothing to do except to maintain itself. It is a case of ourselves being memory. Memory as a concept is what we have chosen to be and that is what we are. We will continue to be this until we are not interrupted by a gift of reality, or, to put it in another way, until there is a free response to our memory, which we will know by the fact that it does not interrupt our memory but it blends in with it and becomes one with it, so that we may continue to remember there unabated. What we have then is a gift of reality, or a given truth, which radiates its own sphere of enlightenment for us, being as much part of us as we of it, and all of this due initially to our memory there.

> Too many burdens press me.
> Even in this darkness I feel
> some sense must be possible.
> Roses are being thrown
> and a curse circles my house.
>
> What have I done to deserve
> the fast decay of friendship?

My father knows where I am,
that much must do me now.
Meanwhile this time too passes.

Due to our memory but not caused by it. – A transubstantiation towards ground. – The ideal of the body of knowledge realized.

One could write at length now on the 'radioactivity', the activity in the round of such a gift of reality; and all the terms one commonly associates with that extinct discipline, (or completely ignores depending on one's professional interest) could very sensibly be taken over and used live. This would illustrate better than anything else what is meant by final terms, because it cuts so obviously right across the artificial boundaries so disingenuously set up and jealously preserved between the professions, and the fact that in the present case we touch on the physicist's or the chemist's terrain is only incidental. The theologian, the artist or the psychiatrist would do as well.

These final terms then make up what we might call the forward thrust of the language that recognizes no borders of the specialist language, not because it makes up yet another set of universalist, abstract rules for expression, linguistically, mathematically or however, but because each and every word, no matter who has used it or to what end, can also be a realization of the word, and the word is not an ideal but a person. It is the person in whom we all share our personality and in order to be most uniquely and specially and perfectly ourselves we must become most thoroughly one with that person rather than setting ourselves most critically apart from him. For we know now what we remember and why we remember and in final terms we really remember him.

When we remember him we do ourselves the most splendid of services. Our memory, as we said, contains a critique, and this critique is oriented entirely towards ourselves, so that we distinguish, first of all, between what we do and who we are, then between what we do for one another and what we do for ourselves, between what we are here and now and who we are, and so on, however the urge takes us, and if we practice this critique urgently and press ourselves into the task, we will give our memory the most advantageous opportunity to gather in that which is being freely given, eucharistically, and which we take completely and utterly on trust without questioning what it is in particular or where it comes from or why *we* should be receiving it rather than someone else.

The one we remember returns to us even as he was in the beginning. He returns, and we who follow him return with him, while we who wait for him receive him.

* * * * *

Index of section headings:

*

www.ingramcontent.com/pod-product-compliance
Lightning Source LLC
Chambersburg PA
CBHW060458290526
45791CB00001B/170